Harry Bamford

Bristol Rovers' First Gentleman of Football

By Hilary Lewis with Joyce Woolridge

Including The Harry Bamford Memorial Trophy

By Steve Sutor

For Uncle Alan, my mother Violet and sister Julie.
For Aunties Eunice and Joyce.

Hilary Lewis

Harry Bamford:
Bristol Rovers' First Gentleman of Football
First published 2017 by Tangent Books

Tangent Books
Unit 5.16 Paintworks, Bristol BS4 3EH
0117 972 0645
www.tangentbooks.co.uk
richard@tangentbooks.co.uk

ISBN 978-1-910089-67-5

By Hilary Lewis, Joyce Woolridge and Steve Sutor

Design: Joe Burt (www.wildsparkdesign.com)

A CIP record of this book is available at the British Library.

Printed in the UK by Hobbs the Printers Ltd

Cover image: Harry Bamford in Charles Buchan's Soccer Gift Book
1958-1959 with permission from Soccer Attic

Every effort has been made to trace copyright holders and to obtain their permission for the use
of copyright material. The publisher apologises for any errors or omissions and would be grateful
if notified of any corrections that should be incorporated in future reprints or editions of this book.

Harry in the thick of the action at Eastville in 1957 against Bristol City as Ron Nicholls punches clear

Contents

Foreword by John 'Josser' Watling

I had the privilege of playing in the same team as Gentleman Harry Bamford, as I think of him now. I can't say that I knew him very well, as he was such a quiet man. He wouldn't say boo to a goose and kept himself to himself. He was completely dedicated to his football and set an example for everyone. He would never just clear the ball, he had to dribble it out even of his own penalty area – you'll read the story of how that got him into hot water in a match against Exeter in this book, so I won't spoil it for you. It was something he was never allowed to forget. I was, of course, part of the Rovers side which won promotion to Division Two in 1953; I am proud to remember how, when the team appeared to be faltering at the last hurdle, it was 'Send for Joss' and I was drafted in to help get us over that bad patch to win the Championship.

If people ask me what was the biggest strength of that side, I have to say it was the remarkable team spirit. Tanny (Bert Tann, the manager) would drum into us: 'When you see one of your team mates having a hard time, get over there. Because next week it might you needing his help.' When we went off to Weston-super-Mare for special training by the sea, we had a great time. Tanny loved nothing better than a sing song in the evenings. My mother had a portable organ which we took down to Weston and everyone would have to furnish us with a song. Tanny gave us 'Maybe it's because I'm a Londoner' and even quiet Harry Bamford was willing to oblige. His choice was the comic song 'The Spaniard that Blighted My Life' which Al Jolson had made popular. The singer swears revenge on Alfonso Spagoni for stealing his intended future wife with the memorable chorus: 'He shall die, He shall die, He shall die tiddly-eye-tie-tie-tie-tie-tie-tie-tie! He shall die! He shall die! For I'll raise a bunion on his Spanish onion, If I catch him bending tonight!' When we had our summer camp at Uphill after Tanny came back from the World Cup in 1954 full of fresh ideas, he decided we needed to eat piles of salad. By the end of the week, we were sick of it. I've never eaten salad since.

Another thing you'll read about in the book is the so-called 'Players' Committee', though we never called it that. Harry, Ray Warren, Geoff Fox, Vic Lambden, Frank Allcock and yours truly would discuss various team matters with Bert Tann on a regular basis. And we did more than just advise about changing the soap for the team baths (see chapter 8)! We would help to decide on tactics and, when Tanny was laid up in hospital with thrombosis in his leg, we picked the team. We gathered round his bed in Frenchay to talk it over with him. I was often described as a 'natural comedian' and the 'team joker', but that didn't mean I wasn't serious about my football. I was always able to lift the mood with a joke, something which every dressing room needs. And, yes, I did give Alfie Biggs the nickname 'The Baron'.

Although I started out as a speedy winger, scoring occasional goals - what the papers called 'Josser's specials' – but more often creating openings for the other forwards, I changed my position in the Autumn of 1956 to become eventually Harry's opposite number at left-back where I spent a happy season or so playing alongside him. The understanding we built up on the pitch is something which I feel is sorely missing in today's game. I don't hear players talking to each other like we did. If Harry or I wanted to go forward we would shout 'Stay', so the others could cover. It was as if we were joined by an invisible string: one would go forward while the other went back. It's not easy to do: much practice and discipline are needed. We'd let our team mates know if they were in space by shouting 'Time'.

Tanny found other uses for his full-backs. He asked me round to his Rovers' house to paint his ceiling and when I got there I was flabbergasted to see Harry building a wall round the back. 'What are you doing building a wall?' I asked him. 'I'm a bricklayer,' he told me, which most of us didn't know, though Tanny had obviously found out.

We were a proper team and Harry was at the centre of it. When we

Josser tickles the ivories for a Rovers sing-song

learnt the news of his death Eastville went completely quiet. There was nothing, just sadness. Then we had to pick ourselves up for the next game. Harry would have understood that better than anyone.

And now I've been presented with the Harry Bamford Memorial Trophy myself, though I can't claim never to have been spoken to by a referee! I think Harry was the best footballer I ever had the privilege of playing alongside. I am sure that if he had played for a more fashionable club he would have been selected for England. I hope you enjoy reading his story as much as I enjoyed being a part of that wonderful Rovers team.

Introduction
by Hilary Lewis

So you may be listening to a programme where the interviewer asks: 'And who from history would you most like to have met?' and if it were me like a shot I know what I would reply, 'Well, my father'.

Of course I did meet him. But I was just three years old when he was killed in the road accident and I grew up being one of the two people who would have most liked to have known him. My sister Julie was born five weeks after his death and she too must have felt the same as I did. We were aware that our background was unlike that of our friends, all of whom as far as we knew had fathers. When we were at school or out and about, if we were asked for our surname and we replied 'Bamford' there was very often a pause before we would hear: 'Oh, you're not related by any chance to…?' We would sense where this was leading and squirm a little knowing the embarrassment which would follow, and hope that we didn't let it be known that we knew very little about the father that everyone else seemed to know so much better than ourselves. We were fortunate, though, that the comments which usually followed were those of admiration so we never really knew whether to feel sorry for ourselves or to feel proud to have had such a Dad.

As children Julie and I had shared the usual squabbles but as we became teenagers sport became important to us leading us both to play for the same women's football team. Our mother was not best pleased by this as I think that she considered it to be 'unladylike'. She had little interest in football and I also believe that she held football to blame for the death of her first husband (Harry Boon) and later that of my father. As a result she did not offer much in the way of encouragement, but as we were inclined to be a bit rebellious this suited us fine.

So many years later those feelings of loss have been revived. Julie was killed in a road accident in 1975 when she was almost 17 with the same injury as my father (laceration of the brain). My mother too died in 2006 (she had never remarried) and then more recently my Dad's younger brother Alan, Uncle Alan, who idolised my Dad and had moved to live next door after my father's death.

I was at work when I received a message: 'Can you ring Steve Sutor? Something about the Woodcock Shield?' I rang Steve and he came to the house to talk about my Dad's schoolboy exploits in the Woodcock Shield football competition. After showing him some photos and my Dad's caps and medals, I remarked that there used to be a Harry Bamford Memorial Trophy. Steve's book *Every Schoolboy's Dream - The Story of the Woodcock Shield* was published; I had a copy. Then Steve got in touch again. 'Do you know what happened to the Trophy?' he asked. 'No,' I replied, 'I tried to find out but was told it was lost in the fire at Eastville in 1980.'

You can't keep the name of Bamford out of Bristol football for long.

Hilary, 17-year-old daughter of Harry Bamford, the late Rovers full-back, has been one of the stars of Compton Wanderers girls team for a couple of seasons.

Now the Women's Western League club have signed up Harry's younger daughter, 14-year-old Julie.

The signing comes just before the most important match the Wanderers have ever played. At the Crown Fields, Keynsham, this Sunday, they take on Southampton Ladies in the regional final of the national knock-out cup competition.

Hilary, who has played for the league representative side and had an England trial, will be on the left wing.

In my picture above, new signing Julie is on the left.

Belles of the Ball: Julie and Hilary follow in their father's footsteps

The next week a message arrived from Steve. 'I've made a replica. I think it would be good to get the Trophy going again. What do you think?' I wasn't going to say: 'No, I don't agree with that,' so I mumbled something like, 'Well, okay,' whilst privately feeling a bit bemused by the whole idea.

Naturally, I knew that my father had been a 'Rovers Great' but was extremely unsure if anyone would care a hoot about an old Trophy and a forgotten player. I was wrong on both counts, which just proves that sometimes it is nice to be wrong.

What had not been clear to me was that there were people still around who remembered Harry Bamford. Some could tell me exactly where they were and what they were doing when his accident was announced on the radio, others the numbers attending his funeral, the skill he displayed in a particular match, his dribbling of a tennis ball or the racing pigeons he kept in the back yard. Above all, people remarked on his character, his dedication to his football, the integrity he and the rest of the Bristol Rovers team of that time showed and that he was quiet, reserved and a strong family man off the pitch.

Reviving the Memorial Trophy, however, has not only brought back memories of my Dad. It has recognised those individuals in the city who have given the game so much either as a professional or as an amateur player, but all of whom had to have shown integrity, sportsmanship and gentlemanly conduct on and off the pitch. What today's hardened Rovers and City fans perhaps do not realise is that behind the scenes each club has a great respect for the other and that in times gone by Bristol's football fans would watch whoever was at home on a Saturday. So the awarding of the Trophy is an acknowledgement of that cross-city, shared respect for football.

It has therefore been an absolute pleasure to meet the recipients of the Trophy and in many cases their families too and to have had the support of both Bristol Rovers and Bristol City to make the reinstatement of the Trophy possible. Of course it has also made me even more proud to have been Harry Bamford's daughter, as the whole process has been a journey of discovery about him.

I would in particular like to acknowledge my gratitude to the following people, for their support, kindness, generosity and encouragement.

Firstly, thanks to my family, husband Geoff, children Jessica and James, as well as my extended family who helped provide photos and memories of my Dad, especially Auntie Mavis and my cousin Pat.

From Bristol Rovers, my special thanks go to Ron Cocks, Mike Locke, Nick Higgs, Steve Hamer, Wael Al Qadi, Ian Holtby, Rod Wesson, Dave Sams, Keith Brookman, Clare McDonagh, Nick Day, Lance Cook,

Barry Bradshaw and Josser Watling. Mike Jay has generously provided extra material and read through the manuscript, along with his colleague Stephen Byrne, correcting many errors and giving helpful suggestions.

From Bristol City, Marina Dolman (MBE), Stephen Lansdown (OBE), David Lloyd, Joanne Robb and Mike Adams could not have been more welcoming.

Jill James kindly gave permission for us to use her father Bob Bennett's wonderful cartoons. Thanks also to the staff at Bristol Central Reference Library where much of the research for this book was done.

That this book looks so handsome is thanks to the enthusiasm and vast experience of its ever-patient gashead editor and publisher, Richard Jones of Tangent Books, and the talented Joe Burt of Wild Spark design.

The eloquent Joyce Woolridge put my father's story into words. Joyce has enlightened me on so many aspects of his life about which I didn't know. I will be forever truly grateful for her dedication, kindness and good humour.

Lastly, thanks to Steve Sutor, whose boundless enthusiasm and love of all things to do with Bristol football past and present began the whole project which has brought the name and achievements of my Dad to a new generation.

There will be more about the Trophy and presentations in Part 2 of this book, researched and compiled by Steve Sutor, but first here is the story of why Harry Bamford's name became a byword for sportsmanship and why he richly deserves the accolade which was given him in one obituary after his untimely death in 1958 of 'Bristol's First Gentleman of Soccer'. The meaning of the term 'First Gentleman' might need explanation for some readers: it means the foremost man of a group or profession and this fits my father perfectly, as one of the greatest gentlemen of football. The book has been based on the newspaper cuttings, personal documents, photographs and other items passed down to me by my grandmother Daisy and my mother Violet, as well as personal memories from the family and others who knew him and saw him play.

CHAPTER 1

Growing up in the 'Hotbed of Soccer'

Mr. Gilbert Baldwin, sports teacher at St. Silas School in St Philip's Marsh in Bristol, was on duty in the playground one lunch time in 1929. Mr. Baldwin was a football enthusiast and a shrewd spotter of football talent, but even he was amazed as he watched one of the nine year olds dribbling in and out of his classmates before scoring a goal in the painted goalmouth on the canteen wall. When the whistle blew for the start of lessons, Mr. Baldwin approached the boy, asked him his name and if he would like to play for the school team. 'Yes, sir,' came the eager reply, 'I love football, but I don't have any boots.' Mr. Baldwin told him not to worry, as he would lend him a pair until he could buy his own.

The exciting prospect was Harry Bamford, who impressed again when he came to football practice in the gym after school the next Tuesday, but the two goals he scored were not enough for Mr. Baldwin. 'If you're going to play in the team,' he told the youngster, 'you must be able to use your left foot as well as your right.' Harry was the type of boy who never needed to be told something twice if the advice was sound. The next day Mr. Baldwin saw him kicking a tennis ball around in the playground - with his left foot.

Harry was thrilled to see his name at No. 9 on the team sheet pinned on the school notice board for the forthcoming Saturday morning match at the Dings against Air Balloon School. But he knew he would quickly have to buy some boots of his own, as his borrowed pair was too tight and the nails which held on the studs poked through the sole. Boots were two shillings to buy second hand and five shillings brand new, a mere 20p and 50 pence in modern coin, but in those days it took Harry four weeks of saving up his paper round earnings and doing odd jobs for neighbours to scrape together enough for the cheapest option. Thanks to the intervention of his uncle, who made up the rest, he was able to take to the field in the first round of the Intermediate Woodcock Shield, a junior schools trophy, against Two Mile Hill School at Kingswood, in spanking new leather boots. St. Silas won 5-0, and Harry scored. Then the team put on their shoes and walked all the way back home down Troopers Hill and along the Feeder Canal.

Henry Charles Bamford was born on 8 February 1920 in St. Philip's Marsh, an area which became celebrated as a 'hotbed of Soccer' and a 'nursery for footballers'. The Marsh was a unique working-class community, composed of tightly packed blocks of streets where terraced houses with no bathrooms and outside lavatories stood alongside various factories and other businesses spewing out plentiful fumes from the manufacture of paint and varnish, animal feed and glue, and the St Philip's Marsh Goods and Engine sheds. Nicknamed 'The Island', as it lay between the Feeder Canal and the River Avon, it was home to 6,000 inhabitants. The eldest of three boys, Harry grew up in 13, Moor Street (demolished with the rest of the housing when the Marsh was reclassified as an industrial area in 1961), with his parents Henry J. Bamford, also called Harry, his mother Daisy (nee Bartlett) and brothers Ron and Alan. Henry J. worked as a labourer and kept racing pigeons in the backyard in cages next to the outside lavatory, a passion which Harry inherited. An acquaintance of the family, aged 93, remembered Harry and his dad toasting bread in front of the open fire which was then crushed and fed to the birds. When the pigeons came back to the loft, he was amazed by the two men's ability to recognise which of the birds belonged to each of them, saying 'That's one of yours, that's mine,' as they flew past.

A studio photograph of Harry as a small child, maybe three or four years old, shows him to be already a sturdy boy, holding himself straight on strong legs. But the positioning of his feet hints at his future athleticism and grace. Certainly, as he grew older he began to distinguish himself for his sporting prowess. An anonymous letter sent to George Baker

Sturdy but graceful: Harry aged three or four   Smart schoolboy

Schoolboy medals: three Woodcock Shield and one League Shield winner's medals and one, far right, inscribed: F.B.O.B.S., Jeffrey Cup, R-up, 1932, which is something of a mystery

St. Silas' Woodcock Shield-winning team of 1932, with Harry, arms folded, front left.

of the Bristol *Evening World* in March 1947 by 'an admirer of Harry Bamford' who had followed his career since his schoolboy days claimed: 'Beyond all reasonable doubt Harry must be the proud possessor of more medals, cups and awards than anyone in our town… Football was not his only hobby as he has won medals for cricket, swimming and rugby.'

The awards which survive from Harry's boyhood exploits are his football medals and caps. St. Silas' school teams enjoyed remarkable success, first winning in 1928 the 'double' of the League Shield and Woodcock Shield, a knockout competition for Bristol and South Gloucestershire Schools. St. Silas went on to win the League another three times, and the Woodcock Shield three times in four years, only narrowly beaten in the 1931 final. Harry was a Shield winner in 1932, was part of the double League and Shield winning side in 1933 and added another League winner's medal to his collection in 1934. His team mates included Ernie Jones, who joined Bristol City before the war, and William Boon, who would later become a police constable and a brother-in-law of Harry's wife from her first marriage. Harry was the St. Silas centre-forward and a prolific goal-scorer. He once netted 13 goals in a Saturday morning match against Emmanuel School. The match report in the *Evening Post* of the April 1932 Shield final, watched by over 3,000 spectators, tells us that Harry had brought his shooting boots, as Luckwell School were beaten 3-0 at Eastville: 'Bamford opened the scoring after a quarter of an hour's play with a clever goal', before getting his second three minutes from time. He caught the eye of 'The Traveller' (long-serving Bristol football reporter and columnist Bill Pinnell) who commented: 'He certainly knew what to do with the ball and generally made direct tracks for the Luckwell goalkeeper.' The opposing centre-forward was a future Rovers team mate and captain, Ray Warren.

Both photographs of the victorious St Silas teams of '32 and '33 are revealing about Harry's character. Even then, he liked to stay apart from the crowd and has positioned himself on the end of the row both times. In the '32 photo, which was taken before the boys had time to wash, his knees are free from mud, as are his socks, in contrast to those of some of his team mates. As an adult player, Harry became renowned for his balance and staying on his feet.

One schoolboy achievement of which Harry was particularly proud was his three caps for Bristol Boys. He was capped in three successive seasons, captaining the side for the last one, a feat which the newspaper claimed was never beaten, which is correct, though Ernie Jones matched it. Although prone to reticence in interviews, Harry often mentioned this and was pictured in newspapers with his Bristol Boys caps on display.

When Harry left school, probably aged 14, he went to work in George's Brewery in Old Market, where he played at centre-forward and inside-right for the brewery team in the Bristol and District League (see photograph on page 22). It appeared that Harry was taking the first steps to converting his early promise into a career in football when he signed amateur forms for Ipswich Town, following a recommendation by Ipswich's Bristol scout, Fred Hyde. Family lore has it that Harry's forms from Ipswich dropped through the letterbox at the same time as he was recruited for a far more serious 'game'. Harry himself in an interview in 1954 recalled, 'I never got anywhere near Ipswich. Instead I signed as an amateur for Bristol City'. Also working at the brewery was former Bristol City wing-half, Bert Neesam, who was a member of the team which had won promotion to the Second Division in 1927 and he had recommended Harry to the City. The anonymous letter-writing admirer quoted earlier remembered that Harry had played for the 'Old Professionals' (ex-City players) against a Bristol City team sometime in 1937-38 at a charity match on the Netham Ground and had helped the 'old 'uns' to victory with two goals. Neesam had also turned out for the veterans and was impressed. Harry then played a few games for the Bristol City Colts at the end of the 1938-39 season.

Whether they were accompanied by his Ipswich amateur forms or not, what is certain is that Harry's nascent football career was about to be stopped before it started, as through the Moor Street letterbox came his call up papers for the Army. On the outbreak of war on 3 September 1939, the National Service Act brought in conscription for

Harry (right) captaining Bristol Boys, shaking hands with Bert
Winters who later played centre-half for Rovers

7-a-side rugby medal, 20 October 1940   Harry's three Bristol Boys caps

all men between the ages of 18 to 41 years old. Harry was enlisted into the First Battalion of the Gloucestershire Regiment, which was sent out to Burma. Initially, men under 20 years of age were not liable to be sent overseas, so Harry, who was 19 when hostilities commenced, was stationed somewhere in the West Country.

Piecing together what happened to Harry in the war is not easy; there are only a few photographs and a couple of other documents in the family's possession. The rather sketchy outline which follows is dependent upon snippets of information in newspaper interviews and columns, which, naturally, focus on Harry's sporting experiences. There is a great deal which we don't know.

Two photos show the teenage Harry in his new uniform. One is a group shot which was made into a postcard and was taken in Newton Abbot and there is also a medal with a shield inscribed '7 a-side' on the face and the inscription: 'Newton Abbot, 20-10-1940' on the reverse, which presumably means that he was playing rugby for the Army there in that year.

Unlike during World War One, professional sportsmen were seen as too valuable as fund-raisers and morale-boosters to send to the front as combatants and football continued to be played domestically, although all professional footballers' contracts were suspended and the Leagues and FA Cup were replaced by various regional leagues and special wartime cup competitions. Many professionals became Army PT instructors. Harry, of course, was not part of this, but he was in great demand for various Forces teams at all levels. Eventually, he was posted to India, to where the First Battalion had retreated from Burma in 1942. The battalion, much depleted by the fighting and by the long, gruelling retreat, was brought back up to strength and spent the rest of the war on internal security duties, moving to Calcutta in 1943. Harry said in an interview that he had three years and eight months active service in the Far East before he came home towards the end of 1945. Much was made when he became a Rovers' regular of the fact that he was a second row rugby forward in the Army. Officers in India, he said, persuaded him to play rugby, although Harry pointed out that during

The Georges' Brewery Team. Harry (far right front) is probably aged about 15

the eight weeks of the rains any other sport was impossible. By this time he had reached his full height of five feet eleven inches (often stretched to six foot by reporters), weighed 13 stone and was both fast and strong.

In an official army photograph, marked 'Calcutta' (page 25), Harry sits in the centre of 21 rugby players wearing the Battalion shirts with the number 28 on them, one holding an oval ball emblazoned '1944'. He is unmissable, given that one of his eyes is closed by a 'shiner' and his cheek is cut, although he seems to have fared better than the chap next to him who is sporting an eye-patch. Two trophies sit proudly at the front. The larger, more elaborate one appears to be the Calcutta Cup, not the trophy currently contested between England and Scotland, but the 'other' Indian Calcutta Cup, the Calcutta Rugby Union Challenge Cup, which is thought to date back to around 1885 and is awarded to the winners of an inter-club competition. That anonymous admirer had also been posted to India and mentioned that Harry had been part of a team which won the 'All India Cup in company with some of this

New recruits: Harry and Army pals in Newton Abbot

country's best players'. This is another long-standing tournament, now called the All India and South Asia Rugby Tournament, but whether this explains the other small trophy in the picture is not clear.

Such was Harry's rapid progress in the sport, even though he admitted that he never really learned all the laws of the game, one Major offered to introduce him to Gloucester RFC. Harry was flattered, but football remained his true love. 'Rugby's all right,' he explained. 'You get bags of fun playing but I prefer soccer, because it's more skilful.'

Not that he didn't play any football. His 'admirer' says, without giving much detail, that he played football for two teams who won cup events and he was the only non-professional in a representative game for the Army. Clippings the admirer kept from the Indian newspapers gave prominence to Harry's performances and described him as 'the best they had seen out there'. Harry confirmed he had played for his regiment at inside-forward and for Combined Services sides against FA Touring teams which included professional stars such as Everton's hot-shot forward Tommy Lawton, Wolverhampton Wanderers' iron centre-half Stan Cullis, both England internationals, and Tommy Walker, the Hearts inside-forward and Scottish international who joined Chelsea after the war.

At some point, Harry fell seriously ill and there were concerns that he might not pull through, but what illness he contracted is not revealed. On a lighter note, he became a cook and was in charge of rations, which he later reckoned to be his best days in India. Close to the end of the fighting, his regiment was moved to the Assam-Burma border and all sport ceased as the defeat of the occupying Japanese army in Burma drew closer.

The British forces did not completely demobilize in 1945 and Harry was one of those who had to wait to go home. A letter, dated 28 January 1946, survives from one of the close friends he made in the Army, a South African athlete, 'Jurgy' Jurgensen, who had gone back to England before him. 'Jurgy' now back in Cape Town where he ran for the famous Spartan Harriers club, said that he had waited as long as he could for Harry in Reservoir Camp, the Gloucesters' base at Robinswood, Gloucestershire, along with ' a lot of the chaps' and when there was 'no Harry' he had to move on. Jurgy bemoans that he and Harry had not been reunited in England, as Jurgy had won an Army championship in the hurdles in 16 seconds without any training and he was sure that he could have got Harry into a few sports 'and won something too. I am hoping you are trying your hand at it when opportunities arrive'. Harry had written to another friend in South Africa with whom Jurgy was in contact, saying that he was considering going out there and Jurgy sent him every encouragement. 'Well, Harry, there is bags of opportunities if you're willing to take a chance, and as you have experience in breweries, there is an enormous amount of work in that line.'

Eventually, Harry did make it back to England. He had been in the Army for nearly six years, four of those in the Far East. He had left a teenager, but was now 25 years of age, a grown man. Many footballers lost the best part of their careers during the World War Two, but it could be argued that the war was the making of Harry Bamford as a future

In the Wars: Harry in the First Battalion of the Gloucestershire Regiment's cup-winning rugby team in Calcutta, 1944

The grown-up Harry in uniform

football star. In 1939, he was not yet making his mark as a forward. However, he had come home bigger and stronger, with the experience of playing more than one sport alongside professionals. The particular circumstances which surrounded the resumption of competitive professional football in the transitional season of 1945-46 also provided opportunities which may not have arisen before the war.

Right Back Where He Belonged?

In December 1945, Harry came back to the Marsh, but he was determined not to go back to the brewery, as he revealed in a typescript which survives amongst the family papers of 'The Harry Bamford Story', probably serialized in 1956 in the *Evening Post*'s Saturday football paper the *Green 'Un*. It was a prospect he did not have to contemplate for long. Competitive football had resumed four months earlier, two days before the official ending of the war, although for a transitional season in which the clubs were divided into two unofficial regional Leagues, North and South, retaining the pre-war First Division, Second Division and Third Division North and Third Division South. Bristol Rovers thus played in the southern division of the Third Division South, rather inelegantly termed the Third Division South (South). A League competition ran for the first half of the season until 12 January, then 16 qualifying matches were played until 22 April for the Third Division South (South) Cup. The semi-final would be contested between the two clubs at the top of each League section. The FA Cup was reinstated, though the format was changed.

Rovers, unlike their City neighbours, had not been able to put together a team to continue in wartime football. Without any income, the fateful decision had been taken to sell Eastville to the Bristol Greyhound Racing Association in March 1940 and lease it back, but at least the ground had not been damaged by bombing like Ashton Gate. Clubs generally found themselves beset by a shortage of players and the difficulties of travel in 1945, as well as financial problems. Guest players were still allowed as they had been throughout the war, but those players in the Army reserve

1381.

Army Form X 202B

CERTIFICATE OF TRANSFER to the ARMY RESERVE

Army No. 5188541   Rank Pte

Surname (Block letters) BAMFORD

Christian Name(s) Henry Charles

Regt. or Corps Gloucester Regt.

The transfer of the above-named to the appropriate Class of the Army

Reserve (see note below) is confirmed with effect from 12 September 1946

*The date to be inserted here will be that following the day on which Release Leave terminates, including any additional leave to which the soldier may be entitled by virtue of service overseas.

Note.—The appropriate Class of the Army Reserve is as follows:—

(i) Royal Army Reserve—in the case of a regular soldier with reserve service to complete.

(ii) Army Reserve Class Z (T)—in the case of a man of the Territorial Army, including those called up for service under the National Service Acts:

(iii) Army Reserve, Class Z—in the case of all other soldiers not included in (i) or (ii) above.

Record Office Stamp.

OFFICE
RECORD
INFANTRY
EXETER

22/6/46

RECORD OFFICER

Officer i/c Infantry Records.

Date

Warning.—

Any alteration of the particulars given in this certificate may render the holder liable to prosecution under the Seamen's and Soldiers' False Characters Act, 1906.

If this certificate is lost or mislaid, no duplicate can be obtained.

Wt. 37285/90   1,000M   12/45   KJL/1516/16   Gp. 38/3
Wt. 40609/240 1,000M   2/46   KJL/1722/32   Gp. 38/3

Demobbed, but still in the Army reserve

had to arrange leave or ask permission to play (Harry was officially in the Army reserve until 1947 and not demobbed until 1946) and the Army, as Jurgy pointed out in his letter, could be inclined to make things difficult.

The Marsh had a plentiful array of adult teams and Harry plunged immediately back into local football. Arriving in Bristol on a chilly December Wednesday, the following Saturday he turned out at left-half for St. Silas Old Boys at Kingswood. Walter Jennings, a member of the Rovers' scouting staff who went on to become their chief scout, was watching the match and approached Harry after the final whistle to ask if he would like to talk to Rovers' manager Brough Fletcher, who promptly signed him as an amateur.

The following Wednesday, 19 December 1945, Rovers had a League game at Selhurst Park against Crystal Palace. Centre-half Ray Warren could not obtain leave from his Army unit. There was a knock on Harry's front door and he was asked to stand in, not as a forward, but as direct replacement for Warren. Given his tall stature for the time and his powerful build, as well as the last minute crisis, Harry's temporary conversion to centre-half made some sense. The first two seasons after the war were ones of considerable experimentation. Large numbers of footballers who never played professionally again, often recruited locally, were given a few games – 29 different players turned out for Rovers in the 1946-47 season and 24 of them were debutants.

Years later, The Traveller looked back on Harry's performance against Palace and claimed, 'He gave a promising display as a pivot', though Harry himself remembered it rather differently: 'The goal came early in the match from the man I was marking'. It was scored after three minutes by Fred Kurz and for the rest of the game both sides struggled on the treacherous, waterlogged pitch in bad light. Harry also recalled that he suffered dreadfully from the cold, having not yet acclimatised to British temperatures after so long away in hot climes. Nevertheless, Traveller quoted one of the London press as saying: 'Unless I'm greatly mistaken, we shall be hearing and reading quite a lot about this lengthy Rovers' defender Bamford'. Harry did not make the team for the next game, a Third Division South (South) Cup qualifier against Bournemouth, but was in the side at right-half (a late change because of injury) when Rovers were unlucky to lose against Aldershot away on 29 December after leading by two goals. 'Bamford,' said the report, 'coming in for [Harry] Smith, gave a creditable display on a heavy slippery ground.'

Rovers, along with many teams of that era, employed a rigid formation which became known as the 'pyramid' - or a 1-2-3-5 line up. Against the Shots, Jack Weare played in goal, the two full-backs were Harry Topping and Barry Watkins, and Ray Warren at centre-half was flanked by the right and left-halfs Harry Bamford and Wilf 'Baggy' Whitfield. The forward line consisted of George Petherbridge on the right wing, Albert Butterworth at inside-right, Vic Lambden at centre-forward, Bob Davies at inside-left and Robert Clark on the left wing. As right-half, Harry would be responsible for marking the opposing inside-forward, the full-backs looking after the wingers. The centre-half was the key man in this formation and was also referred to as a pivot, because it was his job not only to mark the opposition's centre-forward, but to swing or pivot the play from defence to attack by getting the ball to his team's forwards.

In the 19 games he played in the 1945-46 season, Harry was employed in a variety of different positions, partly through necessity, partly because of his versatility and partly because of his attitude and temperament. On 5 January 1946, in one of the biggest victories of the season, 5-3 at Bournemouth, revelling in the freedom of being away from 'the holding mud of Eastville', he was at inside-right, where he set up the third goal for Vic Lambden with 'an astute pass'. Nine minutes later, Harry bagged the fourth - his first for Rovers. In match report after match report, Harry's play is described as 'clever' or something similar. He was a player who engaged his brain and also exercised considerable self-control, rarely letting anything unsettle or fluster him. Later, reporters dubbed him 'poker face'. Such attributes were particularly valuable for a defender, though it was not until 1947 that he first played at right-back, the position which he went on to make his own for so many seasons.

Harry began to knock in the goals. In the first of the Division Three

South (South) Cup qualifiers, a 2-1 win against Exeter, where the players near the Stapleton Road entrance were sinking ankle deep in mud and a squelching sound was audible when they extricated themselves, he made Rovers' first from a cross from the wing. 'A word of commendation for Bamford,' wrote 'Scribe' in the *Evening World* afterwards. 'He is a strongly built young man with a good knowledge of the game and he is a 90 minute player.' He scored the only goal in the second leg on 19 January, pouncing on a rebound from a header against the crossbar and shooting first time into an empty net. In a narrow 1-0 defeat at Torquay on 26 January, his performance at inside-right, although it failed to result in an equaliser, was highly praised, especially his 'menacing' drives towards goal, and it seemed to suggest that his future lay in the forward line. In the second leg at Eastville on 2 February, abandoned just as Ray Warren was about to take a penalty because of torrential rain which even washed away the pitch markings, Harry had his first opportunity to lead the Rovers' attack, and scored after four minutes, coolly placing the rebound from a shot from Petherbridge which had hit the post, into the far corner of the net. He was also at centre-forward against Port Vale on 9 February at Eastville where the players were once again sinking into the mud and scored the second of Rovers' four. Although the *Western Daily Press* reporter, despite Harry's goal, a fierce ground shot which followed one of his trademark bursts forward between the opposition backs, opined testily: 'Bamford did not impress as a centre-forward and held on to the ball too long; in fact there was far too much individualism on both sides'.

For the final 14 games he played this season, Harry was used as a right-half. At first, he and Wilf Whitfield were sometimes caught out of position, but quickly built up an understanding, so that by the time of Rovers' final match of the transitional season, the semi-final of their Third Division South (South) Cup qualifying games, they were a constructive pairing, providing good service to the forwards. Harry's 'tireless' efforts frequently garnered praise, as did his skilful dribbling. In a Third Division South Cup game on 30 March, he helped Rovers finally beat Bristol City 2-1 in their seventh encounter that season,

Team card for Rovers' 3-3 draw at Bournemouth and Boscombe in the League Cup Qualifier on 9 March 1946

thanks to a clever piece of opportunism. The *Evening World* headline declared: 'Bamford Shocks the City', describing how he scored right at the beginning of the second half before the City players had positioned themselves. 'Straight from the kick-off, the ball was pushed out to Bamford who raced to the centre of the field, through wide open spaces… and the Rovers' right-half sent in a flashing shot, which I don't think Cousins would have seen. At any rate the ball was settled well in the back of the net before he turned round.'

Rovers had finished fifth in the League competition and were knocked out of the reinstated FA Cup by Bristol City, but their eye-catching progress in the Third Division South (South) Cup was only halted in the semi-finals by a disappointing 3-1 home defeat by Walsall. Despite the result, the *Western Daily Press* singled Harry out: 'Throughout the game Bamford used his height to great advantage in defence and his many well-directed ground passes marked him as the most prominent player on the field'.

Once the dress rehearsal was over, the return of proper League

A Rovers' team photo of 1946. The players are: Back row (L–R) Jack Pitt, Jack Weare, Harry Bamford, Wally McArthur, Ray Warren, Barry Watkins; Front row Ken Wookey, Len Hodges, Fred Leamon, Jimmy Morgan, Lance Carr

football for the 1946-47 season was eagerly anticipated. Harry said he had kept himself fit in the close season by playing cricket. Across the country, 950,000 people watched the opening matches, despite storms and torrential rain. Rovers' first match against Reading at Eastville on 31 August which finished in a 2-2 draw was in doubt until close to kick off. Manager Brough Fletcher, pulling on his gum boots, was determined the match would go on and directed clean-up operations involving three pumps and 50 helpers, but even then there was so much standing water the ball stopped dead in parts of the pitch. Harry, despite his extended stint at right-half the previous season, moved again to inside-right for his official League debut as the manager kept faith with some of the local talent previously introduced. The *Western Daily Press* correspondent was not impressed: 'It was at inside-forward where the Rovers were found wanting. Bamford had a poor game, and time and time again he tried to do too much with the ball and was robbed.'

Harry was by no means the only Rovers' player who struggled to find his form. Fletcher chopped and changed the line up as Rovers went from 18 September to 28 December without a win and lost 14 out of their first 22 games. At inside-forward for the first seven matches, Harry scored once from a goalmouth scramble on 9 September, in what was almost a stunning fightback from three goals down away against Watford, only for the Rovers to lose 4-3. He was, according to his sternest critic in the *Western Daily Press*, 'still too inclined to dally with the ball enabling the defence to reposition themselves'. On 28 September, he was dropped for the derby match at Ashton Gate and replaced by Doug Baldie to add aggression to the forward line. Harry missed a 3-0 drubbing by a Bristol City side riding second in the table, in front of a record crowd of 25,900, which was squeezed in with the help of 'packers' stationed around the ground. He returned next Saturday in his old position at right-half and fared better, but Rovers, although they took the lead, were over-reliant on an off-side trap which was easily exploited by their opponents Southend United who won 3-1.

After four successive defeats, a fifth was expected when Rovers, third from bottom, travelled to Loftus Road to face unbeaten League leaders

Queens Park Rangers on 12 October. However, their football was 'a revelation' and Rangers found themselves outplayed as Rovers won 2-0, a score line which could well have been much more emphatic. It was a rare moment of light in an otherwise dismal run. Rovers lost five of the six games where Harry was at right-half. One of these was a 4-0 defeat at Ninian Park by the new League leaders, high-scoring Cardiff City, on 2 November, but Rovers were up against it after eight minutes when keeper Jack Weare was concussed and was carried off on a stretcher and they were (in the days before substitutes) reduced to ten men. Ray Warren was switched from right-back to play in goal and 'Bamford took Warren's place... produced his best form, and gave a fine display of footwork, frequently beating three or four men in a row'.

Desperate to stop the losing run, Brough Fletcher reshuffled his team, moving Harry to centre-forward for two games. One was the pasting away at Notts County on 16 November, where an overwhelmed, erratic Rovers' defence shipped six without reply and Harry was considered 'not a success as leader of the attack'. Four members of the Reserves were drafted in for the next game against Northampton Town, held at Eastville in dreadful conditions, but Rovers registered another blank sheet, losing 3-0. Harry came close with a header, but was, along with the rest of the forwards, deemed lacking 'the art of outwitting a defence'.

Rovers' situation was dire. After losing ten out of their last 11 games, unable to score, over-dependent on the offside trap and playing every home game in a leg-sapping mud bath, until it froze solid in December, they were kept off the bottom of the table only by the equally atrocious form of Leyton Orient. Harry was one of those who paid the price and found himself in the Reserves for an extended spell throughout December and most of January. Was his Rovers' career under threat? With hindsight we can see that his demotion was only temporary, but the Rovers did begin to improve without him. They managed to draw rather than lose most games in December and to begin the New Year with their first win since 12 October, but not before they had made club history of a sort on 30 November by being embarrassingly knocked out of the FA Cup 3-1 by a non-league side, Merthyr Tydfil, for the first time since they entered the Football League in 1920.

Harry probably had far too much quality to become one of the many footballers discarded by the professional game after this time of readjustment back to peacetime football. Another factor beyond his control which undoubtedly helped him was the Rovers' adoption in November 1946 of their controversial 'no buy, no sell' policy, with the intention of depending upon local talent bolstered by free transfers and player exchanges. Brough Fletcher and his successor would generally have to make the most of what they had. But Harry was a conundrum in footballing terms and continued to be so throughout his career. He himself always contended that he was a forward rather than a defender. In 1954, he told the *Evening Post*: 'I have always enjoyed my football, but at the same time I have maintained I would have been happier and more useful in a position where I could use the ball more, say at wing-half or inside-forward'.

Commentators in the press and supporters also speculated that Harry's creativity, dribbling skills and ball control were wasted in defence. However, when he dropped down into the strong Rovers' Reserve team he was used at right-back in some games. In the Reserves' win at a frosty Hove against Brighton on 27 December, in tandem with veteran fellow back Harry Smith, he proved himself a capable full-back and it was in that position that he returned to the first team on 25 January 1947. At first it was thought that he was being played out of position, but Harry took a pragmatic view: 'One day, looking at the team list I found I was back in the first eleven as a full-back. To me it was a job of work. I was by no means an established player and frankly I was happy to be playing anywhere.'

And play he did. Brough Fletcher had been finding the first team right-back position a tricky one to fill – four different players had been tried there in the first half of the season. Harry offered a solution, although his first team return against Mansfield Town at home, which Rovers won 1-0, did little to please the *Western Daily Press* correspondent who complained: 'The… change, which was not successful, was the bringing in of Bamford at right-back. His positioning was often at fault and

Calverley [Mansfield's left-winger] beat him with little difficulty... Warren was given too much to do covering Bamford.' The snow-carpeted pitch made conditions very difficult for all concerned, and frequently caused the players to adopt what the reporter termed 'unceremonious postures'.

Nevertheless, Harry kept his place and did so until the season's end. Although Rovers lost

GOALMOUTH MELEE.—Thomas scoring Bristol City's second goal against Bristol Rovers at Ashton Gate, following a shot by Clark which hit the underside of the cross bar and rebounded into play.

Harry on the goal line fails to stop Bristol City's second goal in their 4-0 defeat of Rovers on 1 February 1947.

4-0 to Bristol City on 1 February, they had turned a corner, helped considerably by a settled line up. From 8 February to 29 March they put together an eight game unbeaten run and only lost two of the remaining seven fixtures. Rovers changed their tactics in February on the snowbound, rock hard pitches and played long but accurate, swinging passes forward to nullify the impact of the conditions. In a convincing 3-0 victory over Swindon Town at Eastville on 22 February, where a blizzard raged for the first half, Rovers were so on top that 'it was not unusual for the full-backs, Watkins and Bamford, to bring the ball right up to their forwards and even take a shot at goal themselves'. Welshman Barry Watkins, Harry's partner at left-back and an ever-present this season, continued working in the Engines Division of the Bristol Aeroplane Company and played as a part-time professional for Rovers for nine seasons. The Rovers' defence, so easily breached before, tightened up. A 3-1 home win against Bournemouth, Rovers' fourth successive victory at home, showed the defence at its best and, 'of the Rovers' defenders, none was more prominent than Bamford, who played a bustling, storming game, keeping Tunnicliffe (the home left-winger) in subjection, and at times playing the role of an attacking half-back'.

Harry, as we shall see, never lost the instincts of a forward. In the modern game, where overlapping, attacking wing-backs have become common, this would be an asset, but although the supporters loved his forward runs, the rigid covering system of the day meant that his managers were sometimes not so enamoured. In the 22 March 4-1 rout of Notts County, where the thaw and resumption of the autumn's torrential rain had once again turned the Eastville pitch into a 'morass', a feature of the game 'was the number of solo runs by Pitt and Bamford which left the County team nonplussed'. Easter Monday's game at Eastville against Leyton Orient saw Rovers win 6-1, with Harry and Jackie Pitt giving 'impudent displays of ball control and dribbling'. The 1946-47 League season ended with a home draw against Ipswich Town on 10 May and Rovers comfortable in 14th place, but also much praise for Harry. 'The real star of the home team was Bamford, whose ball control touched the heights of audacity'.

CHAPTER 3

The Best Natural Footballer in Bristol

'Big Harry Liley, all 6ft 4 inches of him, was screaming frantically for the ball. Liley advanced, arms lowered and waiting. With an aberration of monumental magnificence, Harry somehow carried the ball round him and Jackie Pitt. He and the ball ended up in the net. Up in the stand, manager Brough Fletcher pulled off his bowler and stamped on it. "I knew the so-and-so would do it one of these days!"'

This is how long-serving West Country sports reporter David Foot many years later brilliantly recounted perhaps the most infamous incident involving Harry Bamford – referred to whenever his former team mates reminisced warmly about him as 'that match at Exeter'. For Foot it revealed 'the deft grandeur and folly of his ways', how Harry, supremely confident in his peerless ball control, preferred to dribble his way out of defence, 'choosing to beat opposing players inside his own penalty area in triplicate', rather than clearing the danger by cruder means. However, it is more than possible the tale had become much embroidered in the telling. Although Foot commented that the 'extraordinary match belongs imperishably to the Fifties', the incident actually happened in the 22nd minute of a League game on 20 March 1948, towards the end of Harry's second proper season for the Rovers, one that is remembered better for the Eastville club escaping having to apply for re-election to the Third Division South by 0.04% of a goal.

When Rovers faced Exeter City at St James' Park, they had suffered a dismal run of six defeats and a solitary victory. Brough Fletcher had, in desperation, resorted once more to reshuffling his line up constantly. Harry himself, after being ever-present at right-back for the first 28

League games, before the manager had dropped him and then began moving him around, was back in the number two shirt for the game. Liley's appearance in goal was an enforced change because of an injury to Jack Weare. The *Western Morning News* was scathing about Rovers' abject performance, dismissing them as 'the poorest opposition, next to Aldershot, Exeter have encountered this season'. Harry and his partner at left-back Ralph Jones were often caught out of position, slow to tackle and 'easily rattled'. 'Exonian' tellingly saw Harry's own goal midway through the first half not as a piece of self-indulgent over-confidence, but an example instead of 'the panic-stricken state into which the Rovers' defence fell so often during the one-sided encounter' after an almost 'continual bombardment' of their goal.

Harry, the report explains, attempted to pass back to his own goalkeeper, but, worried by the opposing outside-left, delayed and was tackled. When the ball ran loose, in an attempt to cover his error, he ran it into the empty net, Liley having been lured out of position. The *Western Daily Press* was, as was its custom when talking about Harry's penchant for attacking, more critical, saying that he had a 'tragic game' and 'put through his own net in circumstances for which he must accept sole responsibility'. Bamford, it says, had time to clear the loose ball, 'but he chose to toy with it, and the next moment had gently caressed it over the goal-line'. Jones was equally hard-pressed on the left. He failed to clear the ball properly for Exeter's third and handled the ball to concede the penalty that gave the home side their fourth. But all those extenuating circumstances were forgotten as the story was continually retold over the years.

The 1947-48 season had promised much for Rovers, so much so that after an unbeaten first two games George Baker commented optimistically in the *Evening World*: 'I do not think there is any need to fear a repetition of last season's downward slide'. Harry, 'The Man for Anywhere', was 'bang in form' in the opening away draw against promotion favourites Port Vale. 'He would streak over 50 yards, bamboozling five opponents and have a 'go'. Pigeon-flying is his hobby. Perhaps he gets tips on speed from the birds.' But that early promise was

Harry and Ray Warren watch the ball fly into the net for Bristol City's second goal in their 2-0 victory over Rovers on 29 September 1947

not maintained by Harry or the rest of the team. Throughout the first month of the season Harry was being criticised in the press for being too slow, allowing opposing wingers to beat him 'with monotonous regularity'. Even when the inconsistent Rovers registered a rare win, 4-1 against Brighton at Eastville, the reporter commented: 'Bamford has still to strike his best form', while praising his opposite full-back Barry Watkins.

By the end of September, despite Rovers letting slip a 2-0 lead in the last five minutes of their draw against Swansea Town, conceding a penalty which many peering through the Eastville gloom thought had been missed because the ball went through a hole in the net, Harry's form seemed to have returned. October was a better month, Rovers doing enough to stay in the top half of the table, though their home form was poor. When Rovers failed to register a win in their fifth consecutive home game, Exeter City fighting back from a two-goal deficit in the second half, Harry was singled out for a lecture in the *Western Daily Press* after Duggie Regan, Exeter's 'clever little outside-left', frequently got the better of him. 'Bamford dallied too often… [he] too easily forgets that two necessary qualities of a full back are close marking and first-time clearing'.

Although his critics continued to shake their heads over his forays up field, Harry's enterprise could be productive. Against Newport County on 8 November, one of the goals which helped Rovers to an away draw came from his storming run down the pitch, as he beat several opponents before slipping a pass through which was eventually put in the net by Jimmy Morgan. When Rovers lost to Southend at home in the next match, their finishing was 'at times pathetic' and 'Bamford and McArthur had to come up to demonstrate the way to shoot'. Rovers finally gave their supporters an early Christmas present by registering their first home League win since 13 September against Port Vale on 20 December, but couldn't make the season completely jolly by repeating the feat against Torquay at Eastville on Boxing Day.

George Baker usually covered Bristol City for the *Evening World*, but had a rare opportunity to catch a Rovers' game over Christmas. What impressed him most while watching the 2-0 defeat by a well-organised Torquay was the obvious quality displayed by Harry throughout. 'I can only say that Harry Bamford is the best natural footballer in Bristol. That is not all. He places the ball with astonishing accuracy, and frankly, he seems to be wasted at full back. He has his eccentricities, but he rarely loses the ball.' Another wrote, after seeing Harry in the return match on a 'mud-heap' in Torquay: 'I should like to give thanks to Bamford, the Bristol Rovers' full-back, for a wonderful display of ball control under atrocious conditions. It was the best exhibition I have seen for years'. Baker returned to the subject in a special feature, 'The Educated Feet of Harry Bamford', pointing out that Harry was one of 'the cleanest players in the section', so that even the smallest opponent would get an even break against him. He told the tale of how, in one match this season, Harry, marking a fast winger, had sustained an injury after being kicked in the hip, and consequently had to put the ball out of play several times

Praise for Harry in the Evening World, January 1948

to compensate for his inability to run. The referee suggested that Harry should try instead to keep the ball in play. 'Bamford gave the reply courteous: "Excuse me," he remarked to the official, "but I'm playing this game – not you."' But Baker finished by saying (once again) that Harry, with his unexpected turn of speed and strong kick and his ability to beat a man, was wasted in defence.

By mid-January 1948, Rovers were fourth from bottom in the table. What was only their seventh win out of 25 games came on 17 January after it had rained all day at Eastville and they were able to exploit the heavy going against Watford. When his full-back partner Barry Watkins scored a goal from 25 yards out in the 12th minute, Harry took this as a personal challenge and 'the limit of his dribbles knew no bounds'. He got as far as the opposition corner flag, but his one shot at goal cannoned off a defender, meaning that along with Harry Liley he was the only Rovers' player not to have scored all season. That must have irked, especially as one of his goal-bound shots was kept out thanks to a hand ball seen by everyone but the referee. Bob Bennett, known by Bristol children as Uncle Bob of the Pillar Box Club, was a well-known Bristol cartoonist who worked for the *Evening Post* for 33 years. He described Harry's dribbling as 'so tricky that he frequently mystified himself'.

The FA Cup had given Rovers' fans a compensatory taste of success and on 24 January 3,000 of them, 60 coachloads, went to Craven Cottage to see if their team could reach the fifth round for the first time in the club's history, only for second division Fulham to triumph 5-2. Harry once more gave a tremendous performance, refusing to deny his swashbuckling instincts, but never putting a foot wrong in defence.

Another run of League defeats followed, the defence leaking goals. By 21 February it had conceded 21 in the New

Harry's dribbling skills attract the attention of cartoonist Bob Bennett in Rovers' 3-0 win over Watford on 17 January 1948

Year. There was no love lost for Harry's performance ('Bamford, however, appeared to be marking no one particular') in a Valentine's Day 5-2 derby defeat which rather flattered Bristol City, Rovers missing two penalties. Harry was subsequently left out for two games. He returned against Walsall on 6 March, at centre-half, while Warren, still recovering from recurrent bouts of flu, switched to right-back. In the first in a string of six straight defeats, Rovers let in two goals without reply, Harry looking ill at ease as pivot, which took their total conceded to 25 in nine matches. In the next game against Leyton Orient at home on 13 March, Harry began with a number 8 on his back at inside-forward, but was switched to his accustomed berth at right-back at half time, where he was clearly more comfortable. It is not altogether surprising that he couldn't instantly settle into another position, particularly in a team playing so badly, but Fletcher did not have the luxury of giving him time to adjust.

The sunniest Easter for years lifted spirits all over the country, though the gloom around Eastville remained. Harry's personal nadir at Exeter, where he got his goal for the season – at the wrong end – was followed by defeats by Aldershot and Newport County. However, Rovers made a last ditch revival, thanks in part to their other full-back who was converted to inside-forward and who scored in four of their last seven games, Barry Watkins. Vic Lambden bagged his second hat-trick in four days (the first had been playing for the Reserves on Good Friday against Cardiff City) in the match which probably eventually made the crucial difference to Rovers' goal average, a seven goal drubbing of fellow strugglers Aldershot. Despite much improved form, Rovers found themselves bottom of the table, even after an away victory against Swansea, the only club in all four divisions not to have been beaten that season at home, because the teams around them also prospered.

The final two League games of this torrid season were against Ipswich. On 28 April, in the Eastville tie, Harry dribbled from midfield to the corner flag 'past a file of opponents' before putting in a perfect cross into the goalmouth for Watkins, whose header deflected in off the opposing centre-half for the first of two goals without reply. In the League finale at Portman Road, Rovers secured a four goal victory which was the East Anglian team's biggest home League loss ever at that point. More importantly, the convincing win also played its part in ensuring that, of the three clubs who finished on 34 points, only Rovers did not have

23 April 1948: Millwall v Rovers 1-1. Harry leaps to challenge Lions' centre-forward Jimmy Constantine

to go through the fraught and humiliating process of applying for re-election to the League, by the narrowest of narrow margins. The icing was generously applied to the cake by Rovers getting the better of City for the first time in 11 years (although for six of those years during the war Rovers had not played football) in the Gloucestershire Senior Cup Final by two goals to one, the winner courtesy of ex-full-back Watkins. Harry was to collect four such medals in this annual contest between Rovers and City, but no doubt this was the sweetest.

The 'no buy, no sell' policy was roundly denounced when Rovers held their annual pre-season trial game on 14 August and few new faces appeared in the ranks. Fred Laing, a tall Scots inside-forward acquired from First Division Middlesbrough created the only real interest. However, it was 'no buy, no sell' which kept Harry Bamford at Bristol Rovers. Several teams had made enquiries about him during the season but had been firmly rebuffed. Aston Villa were particularly keen on signing him. Alex James, the former superstar Arsenal forward and Scottish international turned pundit had called Harry a 'great footballer' in the national press after Rovers beat highly fancied Queens Park Rangers in January. Ironically, although the disappointed and long-suffering Eastville fans were not to know it, the change in fortunes which lay ahead was to be inspired by players already at the club: Harry Bamford and his new fellow Bristolian partner at left-back, Geoff Fox, acquired as a free transfer a year before, Jackie Pitt at right-half and (despite the fact that the 5ft 11ins Laing was welcomed to give some height to the Rovers' forward line) the 5 foot 4½ inches tall right-winger George Petherbridge in his size 5 boots, finally demobbed from the Army that summer. The lofty Laing went on to make only two League appearances.

All except the injured Pitt were in the team for the new season's opener on 21 August 1948, Eastville basking in the sunshine. 'Bristol Rovers Rely on Old Players' was how the *Western Daily Press* saw it. Those old players were thumped 6-1 by Ipswich in front of 16,314 disgruntled spectators, many of whom left before the end. 'All the old weaknesses have remained,' declared the paper. 'The defence… has as many holes as a colander.' For the final goal, Dempsey nonchalantly dribbled round Harry and calmly put the ball past the onrushing Liley. Two other defeats followed, one in front of 33,747 at Notts County, the glamour team of the Third Division because superstar Tommy Lawton had sensationally signed for them. The England international striker duly took Rovers apart in 'six breath-taking minutes'.

Rovers looked set for a repeat of last season, but defied the critics by winning seven of their next eight games. Marshalled by the commanding Ray Warren, Harry and Geoff Fox began to combine well, Fox knowing to cover when Harry went on his runs upfield. The team began to play high-quality football, not only scoring freely, but, crucially, after conceding 71 goals the previous term, keeping clean sheets. By 20 September 1948, when Rovers had reached the dizzy heights of third in the table after beating Millwall 2-0 at home, the defence had let in only two goals in their last seven games. Weare was so well served by his defenders that he did not have a save to make as the backs and half-backs 'worked to a close pattern'.

There was a rude awakening against Swansea on 2 October at Vetch Field when the League leaders overwhelmed them 5-0, but Rovers, enjoying the stability which came from using the same 16 players for most of the season, were able to recover from defeat rather than drop into extended losing runs like before. Rovers' biggest win this term came against Aldershot, 5-1, the Shots' solitary reply a penalty conceded by Harry after handling the ball. Eastville welcomed the New Year with a 3-2 victory over a Notts County without Lawton who had been concussed when his car skidded on ice. Between 18 December and 18 February 1949, Rovers did not lose a game and were being tipped for promotion.

The team was enjoying its best season since 1933-34 and there were hopes that the club could beat its record of 51 points gained then. Harry had hit a purple patch; in the win against Torquay on 22 January, the understanding with Jackie Pitt on the right which was to be one of the future mainstays of the team was evident throughout, 'Bamford and Pitt,' commented the *Western Daily Press*, 'worked in intelligent union at the top of their form'. He was the star man in the drawn Bristol derby at the beginning of February which put Rovers second. However, while the defence held firm, goals had begun to dry up. By the start of April, when Rovers lost to Aldershot, the Rovers' forwards had scored only three goals from open play plus another two from penalties, and the team had started to slide down the table. The answer was to draft into the forward line the lively, red-headed, 22 year old Bill Roost for the Easter programme. Reading, now in second place, were torn apart 4-1 on 15 April in front of 20,836 enjoying the Rovers' imaginative and forceful attacking, as well as the holiday sunshine. Rovers' second was judged 'the picture goal of the season' and was started by the 'brilliant' Bamford from near his own goal line. Dummying two opponents, Harry pushed a perfect pass along the ground to Petherbridge, who, in turn, played a wonderful ball across the goalmouth for the irrepressible Roost to run home.

Rovers drew too many games to challenge seriously for promotion despite their improvement. One of those ten draws came in the penultimate League game against Norwich, where the visitors overturned a first half 2-0 deficit, partly thanks to a penalty conceded by Harry, 'blocking what he believed to be a scoring shot'.

Pak's cartoon reveals Harry was prepared to stop Norwich scoring by deliberate handball

As a cartoon by Pak put it, showing Harry with both hands ready to palm away a football drawn with a concerned face on it: 'Even the ball could see what Bamford was going to do and told him to keep his hands to himself'. Harry had a hand (legally this time) in the first Rovers' goal after just three minutes, when his pinpoint centre was headed in by Roost and their second was also a penalty for hand ball, converted by Warren. Harry was a clean player, never booked or spoken to by a referee, but that didn't mean that he was a pushover. He could tackle hard but fairly if necessary and he was obviously prepared to stop a goal with a deliberate foul. Handball, from reading contemporary match reports, appears to have been a not unusual infringement which did not result in a sending off like today, and generated many of the penalties awarded.

The draw, 40 minutes of which was filmed for the club for training purposes, ended the possibility of Rovers beating their record points tally. The final League game was a defeat by Exeter City, played like a cup tie, games against the Devon team having an extra edge in those days. Rovers' solitary goal was a penalty – for handball. There was one last match before the summer break began, Rovers easily retaining the Gloucestershire Cup at Eastville on 14 May 1949 which meant a second winners' medal in quick succession for Harry. But although he was hanging up his boots for the summer break, Harry would not be putting his feet up.

CHAPTER 4

'A Third Division Back Causing a Lot of First Division Talk'

Summer 1949 in the Vale of Evesham and the farmers are preparing for the influx of extra workers from the cities, many of them poor, working-class families for which this is their only means of a having a 'holiday'. Accommodation is basic, often sheds from which the cattle have recently been evicted, whitewashed to clean them up, beds are straw paillasses and food is prepared in the communal cookhouse. And the work is hard. The farms grow fruit and vegetables; waiting for the incomers in July will be soft fruits such as raspberries, gooseberries and strawberries and potatoes, carrots, onions, cauliflowers. All need picking by hand. A few acres are devoted to hops for brewing, but the hops on their bines are generally not ready until the end of the summer. Parents are often happy to risk the wrath of schools by taking their children back late in order to get some much needed extra money, though the pay is pitifully low.

Four tanned young men, three stripped to the waist, are taking a breather after loading a lorry with crates of cauliflowers. It is dirty, back-breaking work, but they certainly seem to have the strength to deal with it. One in particular has a magnificent physique, strong legs in which each muscle is clearly defined, a broad chest and a washboard stomach. Hardly surprising, as he is Harry Bamford, and, like his three companions, a professional footballer.

Why was a Bristol Rovers' first teamer labouring on a farm? Harry, like the rest of those who played in English League football, was subject

L-R, Professional footballers Bert Hawkins, Bryan Bush, Harry Bamford and Frank McCourt take a well-earned breather after loading cauliflowers.

'Bushy' manhandles a sack of spuds while Frank and Harry assist

Working on their tans: Harry, two friends John and George, and Frank sun themselves

to the maximum wage, which, since 1901, had restricted the amount professionals could be paid. By the end of Harry's first season, the maximum wage was £12 during the season, £10 in the summer. In 1961, when it was finally abolished, a top flight (and Bristol Rovers were nowhere near the top flight) player could earn £20 a week (the average worker earned £17). Two of his contracts survive in the family papers, for 1952-53 and 1953-54. On 15 May 1952, Harry signed up to a flat rate of £9 a week between 1 August 1952 and 2 May 1953. There was an additional £5 a week for playing in the first team and 'bonuses for wins and draws as the League allows' (£2 for a win and £1 for a draw in League and Cup matches, with more on offer for FA Cup semi-finals and the final). The basic £9 a week dropped to £8 in July 1952 and from 3 May 1953 to 30 June 1953. Presumably the first team supplement would not apply for the close season either. The contract Harry put his name to in 1954 ended on 30 June 1954 and had no summer rate for 1954. The good news was that Harry had a raise in his flat weekly rate – of one pound – to put him on £10 a week. The bad news was that his first team supplement went down to £4.

As a bachelor, Harry was also not entitled to another perk, a club house or flat. So he lived with his parents in Moor Street and had to keep himself on £8 a week all summer until training began again, when the average weekly wage was more than double that. The fields of Worcestershire offered seasonal labouring for the weeks Harry needed it – as well as the chance to be outdoors, where he was happiest, to stay fit and enjoy the companionship of some close friends and family. With him in the photograph is fellow Bristolian Bert Hawkins who had started his professional career as a forward with the Rovers in August 1947, but did not break into the first team. He was about to sign for Bristol City. Failing to establish himself there he was let go. In the summer of 1950, Bert was playing for Bath City. However, he would later catch the eye of West Ham's scout and signed for the London club in 1951 where, after scoring 16 times in 34 appearances, he made a move to Queens Park Rangers. In 1953, Harry would be Bert's best man at his wedding.

The handsome, dark-haired fellow at the other end of the line is

Harry as best man at Bert Hawkins' wedding in 1953

softly-spoken Northern Irish international Frank (known, predictably, as 'Paddy' in the dressing room)McCourt who had first played for Rovers during 1945-46 while he was stationed in Bristol with the RAF after serving in Italy and Egypt. For two seasons he played as a left half-back, before returning to Ireland with Shamrock Rovers, from where he joined Manchester City. In the same batch of photographs is a snap which shows Frank, with a fabulous tan, courtesy of some hard graft in Evesham, looking every inch a star in a smart suit and tie; in another he's in front of a car which would have taken an awful lot of cauliflowers to pay for.

Rovers were aware of how their players were spending the summer and fully approved of this type of healthy outdoor work. When the club released its list of retained players, it pointed out four of them, including Harry, Frank and Maurice Lockier, had not yet re-signed contracts because they had been out of Bristol doing farm work at Evesham for nine weeks, but they were expected back soon. Harry had been fit and available for every game last season; when he was dropped it was because of form, not injury. Undoubtedly his clean style of play would have minimised injury to a point, but the other reason he was rarely injured throughout his career was his physical conditioning, which he took very seriously. Rovers' folklore has it that Harry ate a raw onion for fitness reasons the night before every game. Jackie Pitt claimed that was why Harry generally roomed on his own when the team stayed away overnight, but Harry's younger brother Alan later quashed that story. Harry did, however, eat honey every day, which was specially ordered from Devon, and was a great believer in the virtues of fresh air. When he moved into his own home, windows had to be kept open and Harry would do breathing exercises every day in front of one of them. Labouring all summer would now be banned by modern football managers fearful for their prized assets, but this was a different era and Harry was never afraid of hard work.

An extra, but welcome payment to the players was announced at the end of July. Ken Wookey had been sold for £1,000 and the club had asked the FA to sanction dividing it up between all the players as a reward for the successes of 1948-49. As well as playing in the pre-season Senior Trial game, with a new local signing, inside-forward Geoff Bradford, who had impressed when playing for Soundwell in the Senior Amateur Cup Final at Eastville in May, Rovers' players made up a cricket team to face Stapleton CC for Gloucestershire batsman Horace Hazell's benefit fund in August. Harry, who his brother Alan recalled batted left-handed despite being right handed and once scored a century against Chew Valley, opened the batting, but was bowled out for six runs. Fellow full-back Geoff Fox who was an accomplished Minor Counties player for Sussex, was top scorer for the footballers with 42. Harry was, however, the only Rovers' bowler to take a wicket, the rest of the Stapleton batsmen retiring.

After last season's fifth place finish, the highest in the club's League history, there was genuine optimism at Eastville, even though the opening game ended in a narrow defeat to Port Vale. However, after 10 games Rovers were second from bottom of the League, losing seven times, although they were rarely outplayed. Despite this dismal beginning, Harry was in superb form. 'Pak' drew him as Nelson's column, pigeons, naturally, settling on his head, 'a pillar of strength'.

Nobody, not even Harry, could stop Tommy Lawton, who finally made an appearance at Eastville on 27 August, scoring twice for Notts County in a 3-0 rout of Rovers, pivoting on his left foot to hook a waist high ball past Weare for his first. During the game, eight year old Colin Yeo walked from the 24,794 crowd onto the pitch to secure Lawton's autograph. In the first derby of the season, Bert Hawkins, in

Harry as Nelson's column, with pigeons, of course

10 September 1949: Harry tries to cut out a shot from Bristol City's George Lowrie during Rovers' 3-2 defeat

his second game for Bristol City, made a sparkling return to Eastville on 10 September in front of a record 34,463 crowd, making the second goal for George Lowrie to get the better of his old friend Harry and his fellow fruit-picker, Frank McCourt, who was also impressing. By 1 October, when, in their third match without a goal, Rovers lost again to Watford, who scored twice in the last five minutes, the team was bottom of the table.

Results then began to improve – so much so that by the end of October Rovers had risen to 13th place and taken seven points out of a possible eight from their last four matches. In the away game against Brighton on 8 October, Harry was given the credit for Rovers hanging on to win 2-1 by John Coe in the *Evening Post*. As the home side scrabbled for an equaliser, 'Bamford looked them squarely in the face and refused to be discountenanced'. Match report after match report sang Harry's praises. When a representative for Second Division Manchester City came to watch McCourt against Millwall, Coe said he should have turned his attentions to Harry instead, who was 'everything at once. This cool, unhurried defender turned defence into swift attack by long runs in which he had perfect control of the ball while his service of it to Hodges was as good as any inside man has a right to expect.'

Brough Fletcher counted himself lucky to have such an accomplished defender as Rovers reached the busy holiday period with an away game at Notts County on Christmas Eve, which, thanks again to Tommy Lawton, Rovers lost by two goals. As the Rovers' manager told a reporter afterwards: 'It's a pity there aren't more people in football like Harry Bamford. He's not only the best right full-back in the Third Division, but he's also the cleanest player I've ever seen.' A week later, Fletcher was dismissed from the job he had held since 1938. According to one source, a note was pushed through his letterbox informing him that his services were no longer required. While the Bristol public were still digesting the news, a further sensation was created by an FA announcement on the 9 January 1950 that an inquiry was to be held into the affairs of Bristol Rovers FC. A party of auditors led by a member of the FA's finance committee would be conducting an investigation.

This is not the place to try to unravel the facts behind the investigation, which centred upon what the FA later called 'various irregularities over the keeping of the club's books, including expenses payments to players, scouts and directors'. That extra payment of a share of Ken Wookey's transfer fee was put under the microscope. However, the FA's chief complaint was the tangled relationship between the owners of Eastville Stadium, the Bristol Greyhound Racing Association, whose director Con A. L. Stevens was also Rovers' chairman and whose secretary and racing manager John Hare was vice-chairman of the Rovers' Board. Since 1947, the BGRA had been responsible for Rovers' books. Eventually, at the end of March 1950, the FA found no evidence of irregularities, but put that down to falsification of the Board's minutes and fined the club £250. A new Board was later appointed after a protracted power struggle among the various candidates.

Brough Fletcher's departure after his most successful season at the club appears to have had more to do with matters off than on the pitch. But Rovers had a replacement in the wings who could take over the team with the minimum of disruption. The 34 year old Bertram Tann had been recommended to Rovers when they were seeking a coach to assist Fletcher by none other than the all-powerful secretary of the FA, Sir Stanley Rous. Sir Stanley was a former referee and football moderniser. Since the 1930s there had been voices within football arguing that men from the ranks of professional players should take over the running of more aspects of the game from the 'civilians' who largely dominated it. Rous established and promoted training schemes for coaches and referees. Tann, who had had been a half-back for Charlton Athletic until he was injured while playing as a wartime guest for Southampton, had turned to coaching. Enrolling on the FA course at Lilleshall run by Rous protégé Walter Winterbottom, (who combined the roles of the FA's director of coaching and the first ever full-time England manager between 1946 and 1962), Tann achieved his FA coaching diploma in 1947 and had been coach of the Norwegian international team. When Tann and Rous were in Bristol at the end of February 1948 to watch the FA Amateur XI in action, Sir Stanley put in a good word for Bert to the Rovers' Board and he was duly appointed as Fletcher's assistant. For that reason alone, Bert Tann replacing Brough Fletcher in 1950 (initially as caretaker manager until his permanent appointment at the end of March) made perfect sense as a means of reassuring the FA that Rovers now meant to do things strictly according to the FA's book.

Ever since Bert Tann had taken up the post of Brough Fletcher's assistant on 5 April 1948, declaring that he would do all in his power to develop local talent, he had been encouraging Rovers' staff to attend the FA's coaching courses, while stating his belief that in the future more clubs would be forced to produce their own players by coaching rather than giving into the demands of the transfer market. In the modern game, the appointment of a new manager is an anxious time for a club's players whose futures can become instantly uncertain. However, Tann was not only restricted by 'no buy, no sell', but also his personal philosophy. He was also as great an admirer of Harry Bamford as his predecessor.

The feeling was mutual. In the *Green 'Un*'s 'Harry Bamford Story', Harry recalled: 'Until Bert Tann arrived at Eastville we had no system and were left to play very much as we liked. He made us work in training to a particular pattern and by continued practice his ideas began to bring in more points and we found ourselves enjoying our game more.' But, despite his admiration for Tann, Harry appeared to have set his sights on a move away from his local club. In an interview later in the season, Tann revealed that Harry had come to him and said, 'Bert, I reckon I'd do better for myself in a First Division club. I think I'm good enough.' Tann said he agreed with him, but claimed that from now on every Bristol Rovers' first team player would be on the same money as he would be if he played for Tottenham, Sunderland or Liverpool and that every member of the team was on 'top wages - £12 a week, the same as Stanley Matthews gets. Harry Bamford is perfectly happy, and so are all the rest.'

Initial results were encouraging and Rovers were unbeaten between 27 December and 4 March and did not lose a League game at home between 1 October and 8 April. Harry's brilliant form continued and when Tann's first Bristol derby as manager on 14 January 1950 ended 2-1 in Rovers' favour, the papers called him 'a cool and constructive defender' and 'a complete master on his flank'. Tann's influence could perhaps be discerned when Harry made the national papers as a 'Third Division back causing a lot of First Division talk' and the report described how Harry 'a unique ball player' had invented his own training method by attaching a football to a length of cord and practising kicking and controlling it from all angles'. And also when, on 20 February, Rovers beat Watford 2-0 at Vicarage Road with a team composed of local men, aside from the two wing-halfs McCourt and Pitt. Geoff Bradford, who went on to become Rovers' all-time record goalscorer, scored the first of those 242 goals in this game. Surprisingly, there was a short-lived announcement that 'no buy, no sell' would be dropped on 1 February, but any Rovers' fans anticipating big signings in the summer would have been disappointed by the reinstatement of the policy in May, after goalkeeper and ex-RAF commando Bert Hoyle had become the first Rovers' player to be signed for a fee since the war, albeit a small one to cover Hoyle's share of accrued benefit – a benefit being the proceeds of a particular match after five and ten years' continuous service and very important to footballers who suddenly had to find new jobs and sources of income when their playing days were over.

The run of good form temporarily ended as a gruelling Easter programme took its toll. Bert Tann had tried to prepare for it by taking the players away to the coast at Weston-super-Mare for extra training, but it was unsuccessful. Even Harry Bamford missed a 2-0 away defeat by Exeter City on 7 April as he was unfit because he had 'influenza', one of four changes which were forced upon Tann. A late flurry of wins, however, lifted Rovers' up the table to 9th. On 1 May in a 0-0 draw against Northampton, Harry very nearly scored twice to fulfil what the papers called his 'season's ambition' with fierce drives from 30 yards out. A third consecutive victory in the Gloucestershire Senior Cup eluded him; the 13 May proved to be doubly unlucky as in the closing minutes he placed a penalty the wrong side of the post.

Potential International

Harry Bamford was walking along Broad Street in the middle of Bristol in February 1951 whistling happily to himself. George Baker, football correspondent for the Bristol *Evening World* rushed up to him with the news that he had been selected to tour Australia with a Football Association squad that summer. 'Came the Great Big Smile,' Baker wrote. 'It spread over his face, and stayed there for the next 15 minutes.' Harry took a deep breath and said,' This is great news – you can say I'm very happy about it.' When told the squad selected contained many players from the higher Leagues, Harry merely commented, 'I'll just have to show them that the players in the Third Division can do as well as those in the First and Second Divisions'. His only regret was that no other Rovers' players had made the cut.

The Rovers' team, engaged in what was then the greatest FA Cup run in the club's history, were on their way to Hort's Restaurant (still open today) as part of what the papers had dubbed 'Operation Beefsteak', Bert Tann's plan to supplement their diet with meat by taking them out to lunch every day. Food was still rationed (restaurants had a partial exemption) and meat rationing did not finish until July 1954. The Rovers' manager was careful not to cast aspersions on the standard of food served up to his men by their wives and, in Harry's case, mother, but he insisted that meat was necessary for stamina, and on the menu at Hort's was beef, steak pudding or fried liver. When Harry came into the dining room, the rest of the players stood and applauded and shook his hand. Baker counted it a good omen for the forthcoming game against Newcastle that the waitress was called Irene, like the woman bid goodnight so often and so mournfully in the song adopted by Rovers' fans that season.

Josser Watling and Bryan Bush congratulate Harry on his selection for the England tour of Australia

Harry Bamford spent the 1950 close season fruit picking in Evesham with his pals once again. This time, however, Frank McCourt did not re-sign for Bristol Rovers. Despite being linked with moves to clubs further up the divisions, Rovers reiterated that they did not intend to release any players, which they were perfectly entitled to do under the retain and transfer system, described by its many opponents as a type of slavery. Clubs could keep a player in the reserves indefinitely rather than agree to a transfer. Paddy, to force the club's hand, had the option of going back home to Ireland where he rejoined Shamrock Rovers, although Rovers still held his registration – and it worked, because in October he moved to Second Division Manchester City. Harry may have cast envious eyes at Paddy's move, not least because playing in the Third Division South was a severe handicap when it came to a possible call up for England. Harry's supporters argued his case as a potential international, but by 1951 when Harry was called up to the Australian tour, where none of the matches would count as full internationals, only one player from the Third Divisions had ever been capped by England. That was Notts County's Tommy Lawton, who was already established as his country's centre-forward. The tour call up, though, suggested that Harry was on the radar.

1950-51 proved to be another tumultuous season for Rovers. During it they were to break all kinds of records, including becoming the first football club to be investigated by the Board of Trade, Eastville being submerged twice under five feet of water in the space of seven weeks, recording their then longest run of games without defeat – 19 in both League and FA Cup – and, for the first time ever, reaching the last eight of the FA Cup. One of the more welcome events was that Rovers began with a win for the first time in post-war football, albeit by only one goal, in a tight home match against Swindon, Harry nevertheless, during an outstanding display of defending, finding the time 'to wander up the field and send in one of the best shots of the match'. Although the following two games were both draws, he excelled in both, seeming to have the ball 'magnetized' against Aldershot and remaining supremely cool under pressure in a man of the match performance in Rovers' first ever encounter with newly-elected to the League Colchester United at Layer Road which could match Eastville for mud. Harry impressed by constantly trying to use the ball in the difficult conditions, rather than resorting to booting it up field like everyone else.

By 28 August 1950, when they beat Aldershot by three goals at home, Rovers had recorded their best start since the war, six points without a defeat, whereas by the same time last year they had only taken five points from their first ten games. Although they began September by losing the first Bristol derby of the season by one goal at Ashton Gate, two days later they beat Gillingham by another three goals with another clean sheet. In fact, Rovers had conceded only two goals in their first six matches, while the previous season they had given away 11. The defence, Bert Hoyle in goal, Harry at right-back, Geoff Fox on the left, Jackie Pitt at right-half and young Peter Sampson, promoted from the Reserves, at left-half flanking the magisterial Ray Warren at pivot, consistently provided a solid foundation, but the goals dried up for most of the rest of September, Bert Tann switching the forward line around to try to find a solution. When the month ended with a 2-0 defeat away by Norwich City, John Gummow, Rovers' secretary, was left with a huge 10lb iced cake which he had bought at an auction (presumably for charity). He had promised to divide the whole lot up between them for a win, half for a draw. Hopefully the Rovers' boys finally got their cake and could eat it when they beat Bournemouth 2-0 on 7 October, the second goal coming from 18 year old Bournemouth-born debutant Barrie Meyer, and Bamford and Fox giving their best defensive display so far this season.

The first away win finally came against Exeter on 14 October at St. James' Park, Vic Lambden sealing the victory with his 50th first team goal and Bert Hoyle, acting captain for the day against his old side, getting a warm reception when he lead the team out. He had a quiet day otherwise, Rovers' 'Arsenal type padlocked defence' restricting the Exeter forwards to chances which could be counted on the fingers of one hand. The forwards clicked into gear again against Southend, previously something of a bogey team for Rovers, knocking in four goals with a fifth from Geoff Bradford denied when the referee and linesman both missed that his header had been punched out by a Southend back. Rovers were now in fourth place, their miserly defence conceding only nine goals after 16 games. Leaders Nottingham Forest had conceded 11, but had scored more than twice the number of goals as Rovers' 20.

After the 3-1 victory over Plymouth Argyle on 4 November, with Rovers unbeaten in their last six games, in the *News Chronicle*'s West Country edition Cyril Burchill waxed lyrical about Harry's display: 'What a full-back this Bamford is: he headed out a certain goal in the first half; began a dozen or so attacking movements, and in the second half was up in the Plymouth penalty area shooting and heading at goal like a centre forward. And for the rest of the time he blotted winger Alex Govan out.' Two more wins followed, the second against Leyton Orient enlivened by the referee having his whistle and a false tooth knocked out when he took a ball in the mouth.

RALLY WAS BIG THRILL

Bristol Rovers .... 3 Plymouth Argyle 1

PLYMOUTH ARGYLE'S victory-run is over, how it ended makes a thrilling story that will be recalled by Bristol fans for years.

At half-time Argyle were a goal ahead and seemingly set for their sixth win off the reel. They had looked more dangerous and deserved the goal which Tadman gave them.

While the band played the 29,000 spectators swopped opinions—most agreed that Rovers' unbeaten home record was as good as lost.

And when £40,000 Argyle came out again they had a real promotion look. But manager Bert Tann had given his £300 team of "locals" some sound advice—and they, rolling their sleeves a little higher, recalled that they had beaten Southend 3—1 after being 1—0 behind at the interval.

Great day for Bamford

Argyle superiority was soon over. Playing some of the best Soccer seen in Bristol for years, Rovers proceeded to tear the Plymouth defence to shreds. Petherbridge and Bush danced down the wings and over went the ball, time and again, into the Plymouth goalmouth.

The red light started to flash violently for Plymouth. After 18 minutes a harassed defence conceded the equaliser—Petherbridge scored from a movement started by left-back Fox. Soon after Bradford scored the best goal of the match and Lambden made the total three.

Once again the Rovers had to thank their defence. With only ten goals scored against them this season they have the best record in any division. What a full-back this Bamford is:

he headed out a certain Plymouth goal in the first half, began a dozen or so attacking movements, and in the second half was up in the Plymouth penalty area shooting and heading at goal like a centre-forward And for the rest of the time he blotted winger Govan out

BRISTOL ROVERS: Hoyle; Bamford Fox; Pitt, Warren, Sampson; Petherbridge, Bradford, Lambden, Roost, Bush.

PLYMOUTH: Shortt; Ratcliffe, Jones Rundle, Chisholm, Porteous; Strauss Dougall, Tadman, Dews, Govan

A rave review of Harry's sparkling performance against Plymouth on 4 November 1950. Someone was a bit over enthusiastic with the scissors in the section which praises Harry

Attention now switched to the FA Cup, a competition in which Rovers had had little recent success. Their first round opponents, Southern League Llanelly (now Llanelli), appeared an easy draw, but no other team in the competition had played as many games as the Welsh side to reach this stage – eight matches, three of them replays. Llanelly, ambitious to gain election to the Football League, had recruited five Scots players, one of them their captain Jock Stein, who would go on to have such an illustrious career as a Glasgow Celtic player and manager, as well as managing Scotland. The attraction for the Scots was that Southern League teams were not bound by the maximum wage.

The tie looked in doubt when the River Frome flooded on Tuesday 21 November, drowning the Eastville pitch in four feet of water. At its peak the waters reached to within two feet of the crossbar at one end of the ground. The club declared that work would go on throughout the night to enable the match to go ahead on the 25 November. Two fire brigade pumps operating at a rate of 700-900 gallons per minute pumped the water back into the river, John Gummow estimating that more than six million gallons of water were sucked off the pitch. That wasn't the end of it. Peter Sampson recalled how the players knew they would be in for some hard work once the water was cleared. 'It was our job to get a large piece of corrugated iron roped to a heavy plank and then drag it across the pitch to flatten the surface again, It was the only way because it was far too wet to get a roller on it.' Training was shifted to the County Ground, but the Rovers' team were also treated to a trip to see the England versus Yugoslavia International at Highbury. Bert Tann believed that not only should his players be well fed, but they should also be offered some relaxation. Llanelly's players and directors were invited to an 'Eve of the Cup-tie match' entertainment by Rovers' Supporters Club, a performance of 'Oklahoma' at the Bristol Hippodrome.

The pitch was declared playable, but Rovers struggled to convert their first half supremacy against Llanelly into goals when they met on 25 November. Rovers took the lead, but Llanelly equalised from an extremely harsh penalty; the ball rebounded off the referee and hit the hand of Geoff Fox, who could do nothing about it. The replay was three days later at Stebonheath Park in Carmarthen and Rovers travelled by coach to stay nearby at Caswell on the Gower. Llanelly took a shock lead in the 69th minute, Ron Ainge getting the better of a tussle with Harry to square the ball for Doug Wallace to score. Rovers equalised through Bush five minutes later, surviving a late scare to face a second replay.

Harry, who had taken a knock in the replay, had to pass a stern fitness test before the game at the neutral venue Ninian Park, Cardiff, on 4 December. Two special trains put on for the travelling Rovers' fans proved inadequate and a third had to be hastily organized when the second was too full to stop at Stapleton Road. Many had not booked a seat because the poor weather left the tie in doubt. There was snow on the ground at one end. George Petherbridge gave Rovers the lead after 17 minutes, but Llanelly equalised in the second half and for ten minutes Rovers had their backs to the wall, hanging on to take the game into 30 minutes of extra time. 20 minutes of that had gone before Bill Roost's free kick found Geoff Bradford who scored, before Jackie Pitt then made the game safe with a third. It had taken five and a half hours to resolve the first round proper tie; 40,000 had watched the three games.

It was a similar story when Rovers met Gillingham, their next Cup opponents, at Eastville on 9 December. Gillingham took the lead against the run of play, Harry, who had earlier cleared off the line to vehement Gillingham protests that the ball had crossed it, finding himself outnumbered on the right. But five minutes later Bush equalised. Although Lambden gave them a second half lead, injuries to Roost and Bush reduced Rovers to nine men at the end and Gillingham drew level. As neither of the two Rovers' front men had recovered in time for the replay four days later, Ken Gough, a medical student at Bristol University who had signed amateur forms only a month before, was drafted into the inside-left position. The debutant scored, but then Bert Hoyle unaccountably hooked the ball to Gillingham's left-winger John Carr who gratefully accepted the gift, calmly lobbing it back over the Rovers' 'keeper's head. The second replay on 18 December, again at a neutral venue, this time Spurs' White Hart Lane, was Rovers' sixth cup game in 23 days on half-frozen, waterlogged pitches. Snow fell throughout the game, which Rovers won 2-1 with another controversial penalty, carpeting the pitch, before fog descended. Charles Buchan, the ex-Arsenal player and former England international who became a hugely influential football writer and edited the iconic *Charles Buchan's Football Monthly* magazine commented in the *News Chronicle*: 'In defence Bamford was the inspiration. He placed the ball to advantage and was rarely beaten in the tackle'.

Two days before knocking out Gillingham, Rovers despatched

Swindon 2-1 in their first League game for nearly a month, played on a rolled carpet of snow at the County Ground, reporters spotting no signs of fatigue. Rovers could now turn their attention back to the League. The busy Christmas programme lay ahead, but Rovers managed to negotiate it unbeaten, setting a new club record of 17 consecutive games without defeat against Port Vale on Boxing Day, before going beyond that with a 2-1 victory over Bristol City on 30 December, their eighth League and Cup game of the month.

Widespread flooding greeted the New Year when a rapid thaw cleared the heavy snow. Once again the Frome burst its banks, spilling three feet of water onto the Eastville pitch and inundating the dressing room and the board room. The Rovers' Board, surveying the patch of mud without a blade of grass which was the playing surface, decided to call in experts to recommend how to prevent future flooding. As the *Evening World* somewhat acidly commented, under Bert Tann, 'The Harbourmaster of Eastville', ' the team is at its best on dry ground and no longer prays for heavy conditions'. If there was a bonus for the Rovers, it was that their Third Round Cup tie against Aldershot was postponed until 10 January. The rest certainly seemed to work: they were four goals up without reply within 40 minutes. Further records toppled when the same six players appeared in defence for 29 games and Vic Lambden's opener after eight seconds of the 5-1 victory became the fastest ever goal scored in Cup history. The undefeated run was ended when a solitary goal gave Crystal Palace a narrow win at Selhurst Park on 13 January. Despite this, the Rovers bounced back to go second in the table with two consecutive victories, with Harry at his unflappable best away against Torquay United on 17 January. 'Bamford,' said the *Evening World* reporter, 'was particularly prominent in the cool way he stopped the Torquay left flank, and he and Pitt stopped three useful attacks on the right.

When Southend Corporation announced a free brine baths for footballers offer, on 24 January 1951 Bert Tann took his team by 'private luxury coach' off to the seaside resort for special training before their next Cup tie against Second Division Luton Town. Tired limbs and aching joints could find relief in the warm salt water and weary minds be invigorated by the sea breezes. Also included was a night out in London to see the madcap antics of the Crazy Gang in 'Knights of Madness' at the Victoria Palace. The break had the desired effect as Rovers this time needed no replay, beating Luton 2-1 away in a hard fought game. The extended Cup run, however, was to take its toll on Rovers' hopes of promotion. A 1-1 League draw with Torquay was followed by a 2-1 defeat at Newport County. The *Evening World* asked a spectator from the 'one and threes' (six and a half pence today) to write his own appreciation of the Torquay game. John Bennett obliged: 'It's hard to pick out an individual... But Bamford stood out. He's 'Arry to those of us in the one and three's – a pleasantly tough back with a kick like a mule's,' testifying to the great personal popularity which Harry had among the Eastville faithful.

Harry Bamford would have good reason to remember the defeat by Newport on 3 February. Rovers were desperately tired by the end of the match – except for Harry, who had played a 'magnificent game', suppressing the Newport attack on his flank and getting up the field constantly to menace the Newport goal. When George Petherbridge had to go off with a thigh injury, Harry moved up with the forwards – and scored. As the *Evening World* report put it, 'His goal, the goal for which he has strived for almost five seasons, was a beauty, taken with the utmost coolness and precision'. He did allow himself a celebration, a rare smile which spread across his face, before running back to the halfway line. It was Harry's first goal since the 1945-46 season, and came four minutes from time, from a cross on the left which he shot low all along the ground out of reach of Newport's goalkeeper Terry Pope.

When tickets for Bristol Rovers' Fifth Round cup meeting with Second Division Hull went on sale on Sunday 4 February, to protests from the Lord's Day Observance Society, 15-17,000 people queued for the 25,000 which sold out in two hours. Many waited overnight, wrapped in blankets and some of the early birds walked from Winterbourne and Mangotsfield. The special buses which ran later were full of women. As one explained: 'Sunday's my old man's morning in bed and I'm going

Rovers v Hull City, 10 February 1951. Jensen outsmarts Harry and Jackie Pitt

Rovers v Hull City, 10 February 1951, Harry stoops on the goal line to give Rovers a second line of defence behind Bert Hoyle

down to get his ticket for him'.

Hull City were led by their player-manager, the distinguished 38 year old, silver-haired, former England inside-forward Horatio 'Raich' Carter. Many years before, he and Bert Tann had both appeared in an England Schools trial at Eastville, rivals for the inside-forward position. Tann failed to make the grade. This time, when Hull came to Eastville, 'the triumph was Tann's'. Hull's plan was to concentrate their attack on the left, but Harry, who had just turned 29, as one report said, 'quickly spotted this'. '9 local boys,' another said proudly, 'completely outplayed the star-studded Tigers' team' one of those stars being future Leeds and England manager Don Revie. Harry, acclaimed by all as man of the match, snuffed out the threat from the vastly experienced Carter and the dangerous Eddie Burbanks. 'Whenever Raich in his roving moved to the left, he found Harry Bamford... in brilliant form, and was subdued by resolute tackling and superior stamina'. Rovers, to choruses of 'Goodnight, Irene', ran out 3-0 winners, with two from Josser Watling. Tann said afterwards that Harry was the best player on view and that his display surpassed anything he had seen him do before.

For the first time in their history, Rovers were through to the last eight of the FA Cup and the draw gave them an away tie against First Division Newcastle United. However, some Rovers' players nearly had their seasons ended prematurely and never made the long trip to St. James's Park. On 12 February, Bert Tann took a party of Rovers' first teamers, Harry included, to Dursley Town Hall in Gloucestershire where Dursley FC were shown the Rovers' FA training film and given a talk. The players and officials were travelling back to Bristol in two cars, Harry, Bill Roost and Jackie Pitt in the first one, driven by secretary John Gummow. Before the building of the M5, the route back to Bristol went along the A38. That night the fog was so thick that the drivers could barely see and, as they reached the then popular rest stop of the Newport Towers Hotel, now derelict, but which can still be seen from the road, its name partially spelt out in white letters, Gummow's car drove into the back of a lorry. Harry, despite injuring his calf, was the first to react, jumping out of the car and pulling open the front door.

He found the secretary pinned behind the badly buckled steering wheel, and, with the help of the others, freed him and laid him on the roadside. All of them had various lacerations and bruises which were treated in Southmead hospital, Gummow coming off worst with cuts to the head and his eye. More serious injury was probably avoided because both cars were travelling exceedingly slowly because of the conditions. Harry remarked later: 'I've been in some places in Burma, but never anything like this. I thought the end of the world had come'. John Gummow would not forget what Harry did for him.

All three footballers involved were selected for the next League game, a 2-1 away victory against Walsall. Harry showed no after-effects from the accident, electrifying the crowd with a 36 yard dribble, beating three men before squaring the ball to Lambden. Rovers had applied to the Football League to postpone the game, which was scheduled for two days before their crucial game against promotion rivals, Norwich. Norwich had been knocked out of the Cup, and had been allowed to postpone their midweek game, but Rovers were not, giving Norwich what the local Bristol papers considered an unfair advantage. Even worse for Rovers, the match against Norwich was abandoned after 60 minutes because of a waterlogged pitch when Rovers were winning 2-1, with Harry showing 'international form'.

Bert Tann fought back with more brine baths on another trip to Southend and restaurant meals. Harry and Bert Hoyle were pictured tucking appreciatively into oysters at a Southend seafood stall. Bert ran the Ship Inn at Cockwood near Dawlish Warren which became famous for its seafood. The *Evening Post* made fun of the 'Tann plan' with a cartoon showing a fattened up Rovers' side, a rotund Harry in the centre holding a pigeon above verses which began: 'Oh, to be a Bristol Rover, Dining out with Mr Tann, Cutlets, steaks, and soles from Dover – Three-course lunches for each man!'

Harry had his own way of escaping from the immense pressure put upon the team at this time. The *Evening World* ran a series of articles about some of the Bristol Rovers players' home lives. As the only bachelor in the team, Geoff Bradford having recently tied the knot,

Bert Hoyle and Harry tucking into oysters at Southend before the first Newcastle Cup tie

Harry, predictably, was portrayed as 'father' to 22 racing pigeons in the Moor Street backyard. 'What could be more soothing,' the reporter mused, 'to a player in the glare of cup-tie publicity than to move among the sleek-feathered, lightly-coloured cooing birds before he runs with the Rovers on to the field.' When Rovers were at home, Harry explained, he cleaned out the cages on Saturday mornings. He showed the reporter his tamest bird, 'The Fighter', one of only two to have a name, 'who sits on his perch for a gentle game of fisticuffs, battling away with pecks and kicks at Harry's probing fingers'. Harry's mother Daisy posed with him for a photograph and revealed that she had never seen him on a football pitch since he was a boy, fearing that she might lose her temper if the crowd criticised 'her boy's play'.

But Harry's father would have to take over pigeon duties for a time as Bert Tann kept his players away from the cup fever in Bristol. The team travelled up to Newcastle from Southend by train, where 62,787 waited to see 'gallant' Bristol Rovers take on Newcastle on 24 February with the line led by their international striker and local boy 'Wor Jackie' Milburn. The *Evening Post* printed a request for fans not to ring up the office asking for the score. What happened next defied all expectations. The papers called it a 'near miracle' – near, because Rovers held the First Division side 0-0. Rovers had played ten games in the FA Cup, sixteen and a half hours' football, and had matched the expensive stars of Newcastle. Harry, coolness personified, had the task of subduing the dangerous 6 foot tall Scots left-winger, Bobby Mitchell, a favourite of the St. James's Park crowd who nicknamed him 'Bobby Dazzler' because of his immaculate ball control and intricate footwork. *People* journalist Alan Hoby picked out the expensive 'flops' from the cup teams, commenting: 'Bobby Mitchell, £17,500 [then the record fee for a winger] Newcastle outside-left. Had a tough opponent in Bristol's right-back Harry Bamford who cost £10'.

The team were mobbed by 10,000 well-wishers when they returned to Temple Meads station with only a few days to prepare for the Wednesday afternoon replay, hoping to emulate Millwall, the only Third Division side to reach the semi-final of the FA Cup. An estimated

Harry shows off his pigeons in his backyard in St. Philip's Marsh

28 February 1951: Harry guards Rovers' goal as Hoyle comes out to thwart a Newcastle attack

Heroes' Welcome. Rovers are mobbed at Temple Meads

100,000 people had jammed Stapleton Road and Muller Road as they scrambled for the 30,000 tickets on sale. When Geoff Bradford scored after 15 minutes, a famous upset seemed on the cards, but Newcastle equalised through a deflection off Geoff Fox and scored twice more, eventually winning the cup by defeating Blackpool in the final. It was the first home match that Rovers had lost in 10 months

Although Bristol Rovers won their next League game 3-1 against Exeter and the papers commented optimistically that there had been 'no reaction' to the cup run and exit, the team could not hold their promotion chase together, the season petering out in a series of draws and defeats, though there were still enough victories to rack up their highest points total ever. Harry was ever-present in this marathon season, apart from the final game. He also missed the Gloucestershire Senior Cup game against Bristol City because he was flying out to Australia to represent his country, rather than spending the summer on an Evesham farm.

Harry for England

In September 1950, every Football League club was asked to nominate players who would be willing to take part in the Football Association's first tour of Australia since before the war in 1937. Since peace was restored, the Australian Football Association had made frequent requests for an English side to visit their country and this, in the Silver Jubilee year of Australia becoming a Commonwealth, would be the first all-professional party ever sent. Bristol Rovers put forward the names of several players, but only Harry Bamford, as we have seen, made the final 18. As members of the squad would have to miss the last game of the season and would be expected to play 20 games over the 10 weeks between 7 May and 30 July, it is perhaps unsurprising that there were no players from the top six finishers in the First Division. Five First Division sides provided nine players between them: Charlton Athletic three; Stoke City one; Bolton Wanderers two; Portsmouth two and Sheffield Wednesday one. Seven players came from five clubs in the Second Division: Sheffield United three; and one apiece from West Ham and Luton Town. Harry and Leo Kieran from Tranmere Rovers were the only Third Division representatives. The tour was like a modern international cricket tour, comprising a number of matches against teams from the six Australian states and five 'test' matches against the Australian National team. These lengthy summer tours continued until 1978, though by the 1960s they had become considerably shorter.

The members of the tour party all received a small booklet containing an itinerary, a list of flights and a brief history of football in Australia and the previous two test tours between the two countries. Harry carefully kept his, along with a box full of clippings and souvenirs. In the section headed 'General Notes' players were given information about how to join the tour party in London. A rail voucher would be sent and players were expected to assemble at the Great Western Hotel in Paddington on Sunday 6 May and would fly from London Airport in the evening on 7 May after attending a reception given by the High Commissioner of Australia at Australia House.

The FA's parsimony towards players on international duty at all levels was notorious: Wilf Mannion once had to stand for the whole train journey back to Middlesbrough from his appearance in an international at Wembley with an injured leg because he was booked second class on a crowded train and Stanley Matthews was summoned to appear before the FA to account for an expenses claim for a cup of tea and a scone he bought at Carlisle station while on his way to an international game in Scotland. The English FA remained true to form during this tour, which was paid for by the Australian FA. Under currency regulations, no individual was allowed to take more than £5 sterling out of Britain and couldn't spend it either. Members of the party would be provided with an allowance of £1 10 shillings a day (£1.50p), from which they were expected to pay for 'personal luggage, telegrams, cleaning and pressing of suits and long distance telephone calls'. And players had to provide part of their own kit: the FA would provide shorts, stockings and numbered shirts, but the players had to take 'athletic slips, gym shoes, shin guards and football boots'. Just to clear up any possible misunderstanding, the guide stated categorically: 'No bonuses will be paid in respect of matches played'. The squad were, however, presented with team blazers and ties and Harry kept the embroidered badge from his top blazer pocket as well as the three lions badge from his playing shirt.

There was considerable pride in Bristol at Harry's selection, reflected in the local papers which reported regularly on the tour. Harry was the first Rovers' player to represent his country on one of these tours, which were given a 'B' international status, England B teams having been introduced by Walter Winterbottom in 1947 as a way of introducing young players into the national side. This meant that the cap awarded for taking part in the tour was not a full international cap. Two Bristol

Harry's England shirt badge

Official tour lapel badges

The England squad: L-R Back row: R. Langton, F. Broome, E. Burgin, H. Webster, I. Clarke, D. Parker.
Middle row: R. Shotton, L. Kiernan, W. Smith, S. Bartram, H. Bamford, J McCue. J. Shaw. Front row: G.
Hurst, J. Sewell. R. Flewin, D. Wiseman (Manager), F. Adams (Manager), S. Owen, F. Lock, J. Hagan

The tour party disembark in Perth

City players had been on previous tours to South Africa, Billy Wedlock in 1910 and Cyril Treasure in 1920. It was a rare honour for the city.

The tour party initially flew to New York, where a football match was hastily arranged against an American Soccer League All-Stars side, played at Croke Park in the Bronx, which England won 4-0, before flying to San Francisco where they spent a day until the final leg of their journey to Sydney. The first game of the tour took place a week later, against South Coast at the Wollongong Showground on Wednesday 16 May. The visitors were given a hero's welcome; cheering schoolchildren lined the whole of the forty mile route between Sydney and Wollongong. Jimmy Hagan remarked: 'It's something you don't get on the road to Bramall Lane'. Harry got the South Coast team, which contained several Australian Internationals, to sign a programme for the game which was an easy victory for the Englishmen. In goal was the 5ft 7ins Ted Burgin of Sheffield United, the youngest, at 24, and least experienced of the two English goalkeepers, who made up for his lack of height with exceptional agility. The other keeper was veteran red-haired wartime international Sam Bartram from Charlton Athletic, who could give Burgin three inches and 13 years and who became known as 'the finest goalkeeper never to play for England'. The full-backs were Harry and Frank Lock, Bartram's team mate at Charlton, with two of the youngest players of the squad, Sheffield United's Joe Shaw and Leo Kieran at half-back, flanking the hugely experienced Reg Flewin, Portsmouth's centre-half and captain who had won two First Division Championship medals in 1949 and 1950. The forward line consisted of Charlton's Gordon Hurst on the right wing, another Portsmouth stalwart and double Championship winner Ike Clarke (36), who later went on to manage Yeovil Town, at right inside-forward. Frank Broome, also 36 and a wartime international, led the line at centre-forward. Jimmy Hagan of Sheffield United, under whose management Benfica would win the Portuguese Championship three times and reach the semi-finals of the European Cup, and Bolton's England international Bobby Langton completed the line up on the left.

10,000 packed out the ground more used to crowds of 1,000 at the most, delirious spectators climbing onto roofs and up trees. By half-time the visitors were able to enjoy the fine, sunny weather, four goals up thanks to a brace from Langton and goals from Kiernan and Hagan. After the break, Clarke added two and Broome scored the last to make it 7-0. One spectator commented: 'It's a different game the way these chaps play it', and one reporter in the Australian press agreed that the 'English lads [had] paraded all their arts'.

Three days, later on Saturday 19 May, the tourists were in action again, against New South Wales at the Sydney Showground as the last game in a three-match programme, and rattled up another big score in front of 45,000. The gate receipts of £6,505 were a record for a football match in Australia. There were several changes to the England team: Sam Bartram was in goal and Harry's partner at left-back was Stoke City's John 'Chopper' McCue, who, as his nickname suggests, had a robust tackling style which would have been in stark contrast to Harry's clean play. Derek Parker from West Ham was at half-back and

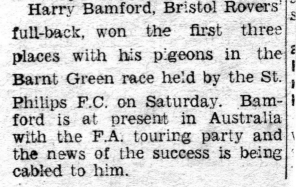

Harry Bamford 1, 2, 3

Harry Bamford, Bristol Rovers' full-back, won the first three places with his pigeons in the Barnt Green race held by the St. Philips F.C. on Saturday. Bamford is at present in Australia with the F.A. touring party and the news of the success is being cabled to him.

Harry was kept informed of his pigeons' winning exploits

Harry poses proudly in his England shirt before one of the Test matches

Luton's Syd Owen replaced Flewin at pivot. Birmingham's Bill Smith was at centre forward. The change which caused most excitement, at number 8, was the inclusion of Jackie Sewell, then rated as the world's most expensive footballer after his recent £35,000 transfer from Notts County to Sheffield Wednesday. Sewell lived up to his billing, opening the scoring after eight minutes and adding another two in the second half. Jimmy Hagan got two and Hurst, Smith and Langton scored one apiece to make the final score 8-1. Harry was not a 'name' and hadn't yet featured among the 'pen portraits' of the English players singled out in the match programmes, but the report of the game in the Bristol *Evening Post* claimed he was one of the outstanding players on the pitch.

R. 'Tugger' Bryant, ex-Australian international, held a post-mortem, with the conclusion that Australia 'can have little hope of winning in the current test series', particularly as, as amateurs, there was little time for developing skills or team work. The gulf in standards was glaring, although in the next game on 22 May, played in showery conditions and watched by a disappointing 5,000, the Australians scored twice. The change was attributed to advice from the Sydney goalkeeper whose name was a boon to reporters, Norman Conquest, who 'may yet be the downfall of the English'. After picking the ball out of his net four times in the first half, he lectured his team mates in the dressing room, telling them to watch the ball rather than the man. The final score was 6-2 and one Australian report described Harry's performance as brilliant, admiring how he 'kept his forwards on the attack with perfect passes, two of which resulted in goals'.

The tour provided the opportunity for an outpouring of nostalgia and patriotism for the 'old country' from English migrants. That night the players were the guest of the Ex-Imperials Sailors and Soldiers' Club for a dinner at Union Jack House in Sydney, the menu for which featured a bulldog glaring at a kangaroo with the motto, 'There'll always be an England'. The fare proffered was sustaining, ranging from oyster cocktail and roast pork with apple sauce with mash, followed by caramel ice cream cake and welsh rarebit. Harry would have had double reasons for celebration, having played well and receiving a cable that his pigeons had taken all three first prizes in the St Philip's Flying Club's latest race.

The Australian papers made much of the attraction of the tour games for 'New Australians' of every nationality when the First Test match against the Australian national side took place at the Sydney cricket ground on 26 May. The *Sydney Herald* reported that one-third of Sydney's Chinese community saw the game and that chop suey restaurants in the city organised their rota to allow as many chefs and waiters as possible to attend. The team was cheered on and the referee barracked in a 'weird medley of languages', the English contingent, it was claimed, offering the 'traditional' encouragement of 'Coom on, Chooms'. 46, 104 spectators streamed into the ground from 10 a.m. onwards, making their way there in a convoy of flat-top trucks and cars. Surviving Australian newsreel footage of the match titled 'Shoot, Laddie!', shows Harry making one of his powerful runs forward. The English won 4-1, a score line which encouraged the Australians but disappointed the visitors who blamed both the hard pitch and the light ball for what they considered a substandard display. David Wiseman, the co-manager of the English squad commented: 'Our lads could not control the ball. It is too light. Wait until the second test when the true English-made ball will be used.' Wiseman and his management partner Frank Adams followed that up with a written protest to the Australian FA objecting to the playing of two curtain-raiser games before the Test on a wet pitch which had already been cut up by seven rugby games played on it in the previous four days.

Harry appeared to be really enjoying being in Australia. He was organising the players to go swimming every morning at Coogee Beach, which, after the Feeder and Weston, he said was like 'jumping into a hot bath'. Thanks to Sid Shortman, a Bristolian serving with the Royal Australian Navy who formerly played regularly for Cotham Sports in the Downs League and who sent John Gummow a stack of clippings from the Australian papers about the tour, the *Pink 'Un* was able to keep their readers up to speed about Harry's exploits. The *Pink 'Un* proudly quoted from *Truth*, the Sunday newspaper with the largest circulation in Australia: 'England have a grand player in Harry Bamford. He had a

Warm weather training with the squad

Harry keeps himself in shape.

ton of work to do, but displayed wonderful temperament to get England out of trouble with his tigerish tackling, good positioning, and accurate kicking'. Another report said the 'man who appeals most to Australian football fans is big Bristol Rovers' full-back Harold Bamford'. 'The Diggers', the paper went on,' are fascinated by his nonchalant manner, and impertinent but clever dribbles up field.' For the *Pink 'Un* this was proof that Harry could hold his own in the best company. Harry wrote the paper a letter confirming that the hard ground had prevented the game being a good one, but also that he had been amazed by the state of the cricket wicket which he described as a 'black area with two or three inches of mud on it'.

The Australians were enormously impressed by the Englishmen's fitness regime, particularly the match-day ban on smoking and drinking. However, there was a long injury list after the bruising encounter, which led to Reg Flewin being stretchered off unconscious after a kick to the temple and Frank Lock was also knocked senseless in a collision. Ike Clarke got away with being 'only' dazed. Harry, so rarely injured back home, had a sore ankle. And five others including Flewin and Lock were on the 'invalid' list. There was no let up in the schedule, however, but the much changed team without Harry still beat Northern Districts 7-1 at Cessnock in New South Wales. The English management were becoming concerned by the increasing physical approach of the Australian teams and the seventh game of the tour against New South Wales on 2 June was marred by the physical 'battering' which was meted out to the tourists. David Wiseman threatened that he would advise the FA not to send any more professional teams to Australia unless the rules were interpreted as they were in England. 'Clubs would never have sent valuable players here,' he said, 'if they had known there was such danger of injury.' The players complained that they had faced 90 minutes of 'kicking and pushing that prevented anyone from attempting to play recognisable football'. The South African referee came in for particular criticism for not penalising 'bulldozing obstructions' and the NSW right-half Bobby Bignall was so embarrassed by an unjust penalty awarded against Flewin that he deliberately shot wide of goal.

Harry's programme for the match against an Australian XI at Adelaide Oval which was signed by Don Bradman

Tasmanian official hospitality for the England team, even if the accommodation was not up to scratch.

The touring team now went south for the next stage of the tour, but on their arrival at Melbourne were unhappy with their hotel, the accommodation being little more than 'box rooms'. Wiseman's subsequent threat to cancel the three Melbourne fixtures had the desired effect and another hotel was found at the nearby coastal resort of St. Kilda, which would have made the daily swims easier. England scored twelve goals without reply in their next two games, both against Victoria. In the second, at the Melbourne Cricket ground on 9 June, nearly 30,000 saw a sparkling display by Sewell who scored all seven, making that a total of 47 in eight games, the defence conceding only six. In the third Melbourne game against an Australian XI, Ike Clarke bagged three of England's six goals and the solitary Australian reply came courtesy of a misunderstanding between goalkeeper Burgin and Harry which allowed an opposing forward to slip through and score. Harry's pigeons continued to do well in his absence, winning first place at Chesterfield and coming second and third at Ripon.

When the tour moved to Tasmania, the press became highly critical when the party again walked out of their hotel. The *Melbourne Herald* claimed that the walk-out had provoked an 'unprecedented outburst of criticism'. One correspondent to a local Hobart paper, revealing his own prejudices in the process, fulminated: 'Now that Government House is vacant it is a pity these petted boys were not sent there, with a butler for each… It would be interesting to hear something of the social status of these darlings of professionalism in their own country… It is to be hoped that any future tour will be by an amateur team, which would probably know how to act as sportsmen.' But the English management hit back, pointing out, 'We represent the greatest sporting organisation in the world and these boys are used to the best hotels'. Although it would have probably been more tactful to say that the squad was about to play its eleventh game in just over a month and could not be expected to stay in sub-standard, cramped accommodation.

The newspapers linked the hotel walk-out with an attempt to sabotage the first of two matches against Tasmania by scattering thousands of fragments of broken glass over the pitch. Officials worked all morning

Harry looks ready for the game

painstakingly removing them and extra police were deployed around the ground to prevent any outbreak of hooliganism. As it was, they weren't needed; the 3,000 crowd was quiet. The English team seemed to have decided to answer their critics on the pitch and smashed in eleven goals without reply, Gordon Hurst and Notts County's Frank Broome both notching up hat-tricks. This was despite finishing the game with nine men, Harry, John McCue and Ike Clarke having to go off injured, Joe Shaw coming on as substitute for Harry. The English team had not finished. On 19 June in Launceston, Jimmy Hagan went one better than Sewell, hitting eight in a 17-0 thrashing of Tasmania. Having picked the ball out of his net eight times before half time, as well as enduring a continual barrage from the English forwards, the home goalkeeper was replaced after the interval. Before leaving to return to Sydney, England scored another 13 against an Australian XI at Adelaide Oval, but this time let in a goal. Don Bradman, arguably Australia's greatest ever batsman, signed a souvenir programme for Harry.

The squad was nicely warmed up for the Second Test at the Sydney

AUSSIES IMPROVE IN SOCCER TEST

Despite their loss by 6-1, Australia gave their best display of the series in the Fourth Test against England at the Sydney Showground yesterday.

The Aussies' defence for the first 30 minutes was terrific.

Clever English winger Gordon Hurst gave the crowd of 9000, who paid £1764 for admission, their first thrill.

He flashed a high cross into the goalmouth which Lord tried to deflect over the bar.

The ball struck the crossbar and bounced out to Sewell who had it in the net in a flash.

After that the greater experience and skill of the Englishmen started to tell.

Broome left the field injured and was replaced by Harry Webster, making his first appearance in Sydney.

He immediately started to hit the high spots. He finished with three goals to his credit.

The Australian back line took a terrific pasting in the second half.

Kevin O'Neill gave an outstanding display and was well supported by Lawrie and Duff.

Bob Bignell put punch into the half-backs.

"Joek" McMahon was the best of the Australian forwards.

He received good support from Parsons and Hulme, but wingers Lake and Robertson had an off day.

Big full-back H. Bamford again gave a great display for England.

Terrific in defence, he also had the speed to move up with the half-backs in attacking movements.

Sewell again was outstanding in the forwards.

Clarke, Webster and Langton could not be faulted.

Goalies Grand

Both goalies were grand. Lord had a ton of work to do, but, apart from an early error, could not be faulted.

England 6 (H. Webster 3, J. Sewell 2, G. Hurst) beat Australia 1 (E. Hulme).

ENGLAND: E. Burgin, H. Bamford, J. McCue, D. Parke, S. Owen, J. Shaw, G. Hurst, J. Sewell, L. Clarke, F. Broome, R. Langton.

AUSTRALIA: R. Lord, K. O'Neill, C. Drummond, R. Lawrie, R. Bignall, E. Duff, K. Lake, E. Hulme, F. Parsons, J. McMahon, H. Robertson.

N.S.W. Team

The N.S.W. Soccer team to play England at Wollorgong, next Sunday, was chosen last night:—

R. Lord, K. O'Neill, D. Wendt, R. Bignell, A. Poole, E. Duff, E. Kemp, E. Hulme, F. Parsons, J. McMahon, H. Robertson.

Reserves: W. Mahoney, C. Drummond, R. Young, G. Russell.

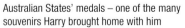
Harry impresses in the Fourth Test

BAMFORD'S INJURY

Harry Bamford (badly bruised thigh) was one of six players of the English F.A. touring team in Australia who were today treated for injuries to get them fit for the fifth Test on Saturday.

The others were Hagan (strained foot tendon), Sewell (injured thigh muscle), Broome (pulled groin muscle), Clarke (groin and ankle injuries), and Kieran (pulled back muscle).

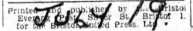

TWO GO DOWN IN SOCCER

England's centre-forward Harry Bamford and Granville right-back Bob Lee both take a fall in yesterday's Soccer match at Cumberland Oval. Others in the picture are, from left, Granville's goalkeeper Ron Lord, centre-half A. McAlister, and left-half Norm Rowlands.

The English players were often on the receiving end of rough play and began to pick up injuries

Australian States' medals – one of the many souvenirs Harry brought home with him

A set of teaspoons decorated with the Australian States' crests

Cricket Ground on 30 June, where, appropriately, they recorded a cricket score of 17-0 in front of 14,000. Harry would have smiled when he saw the pitch. Six inches of rain in a week had left it an Eastville-style quagmire, players sinking two inches deep in the mud in the centre. Frank Broome, one of four players to score a hat-trick, commented: 'We just couldn't help scoring goals; the mud reminded us of home'. Broome and his team mates used their experience of the conditions not to try to play the ball along the ground, but to hit long passes. Jackie Sewell topped the scorers with six goals and Sam Bartram, who kept a clean sheet, sportingly walked the length of the pitch at the end to console his opposite number Conquest with the words: 'But for you, Norman, we would have got twice as many'.

The English team now travelled to the north-east to the city of Brisbane, to prepare for the Third Test in a week's time, defeating Queensland 7-1. The conditions could not have been more difficult, the pitches bone dry and rock hard. The pen portraits of the English in the programme for the Third Test demonstrate what a big impression Harry had made. In the first programmes for the tour he was not mentioned or just given a cursory few lines. Now Harry's profile read: 'Harold Bamford of Bristol Rovers has been one of the outstanding successes of the tour so far. This 6-footer has been most impressive, and his style has captivated all who have seen it. His only representative games before coming to Australia have been as a schoolboy, but if his form on this tour is any guide, we shall hear more of him in International football in the future.'

More controversy dogged the Third Test at the Gabba on 7 July. England put on a fine display of 'fast and scientific' football in front of 23,000, the highest crowd ever for a soccer match in Brisbane, winning 4-1 and taking the 'Ashes'. Australia put up gallant resistance, but their attacks in the second half 'broke down against a strong English defence in which Flewin and Bamford shone'. However, despite playing some of their best football of the tour in the first half and scoring twice within the first five minutes, in the second half the English adopted what the Australians called 'go slow' tactics. Manager David Wiseman explained after the game: 'My lads didn't want to get hurt today on the hard ground. They have had a tough tour, and must now take things a bit easy. Don't forget they face a tough season's football when they get back in a month's time.'

Diplomacy was not Wiseman's strong suit. Those who had paid their money to see the English team were perhaps entitled to feel aggrieved that it was saving itself for a return to the English Leagues. During the game, spectators who had obviously been enjoying some liquid refreshment and were expecting a torrent of goals, began barracking the tourists for taking it easy and bellowing: 'Get on with the game!' Scuffles broke out which descended into a mass brawl, only quelled by police intervention. However, the English players' slackening off was, in their defence, also prompted by robust play by the Aussies which left Langton limping and caused Flewin to complain to the referee, who was having none of it. Against Central Queensland in Bundaberg in the next game they made sure the score line was a more respectable 13-1.

However, by the time of the Fourth Test in Sydney on 16 July, the team was considerably the worst for wear, even though it registered an easy 6-1 win. Bolton Wanderers' 20 year old Harry Webster, who came on as sub, scored a hat-trick despite nursing a damaged ankle and three stitches in his head. When the English players were trotting, or as one report put it, limping, off the pitch after the whistle, they were asked to pause at a table by the touchline. 'It is not often,' the paper reflected, 'that a team wins a trophy that it did not know even existed. But that is what happened to the FA tourists yesterday… To the accompaniment of three terrific cheers from the 10,000 fans, they became the happy but amazed recipients of a three-feet-high representation of the entire globe in solid silver, mounted on four great silver pillars and surrounded by great golden angels blowing trumpets'. It was the Australian Government Jubilee Football Trophy which the tourists were told they had just won outright. Not that they took it home with them. There is no trophy matching this description in the possession of the English FA. Another reward was an official dinner the following Monday at the Black Tulip restaurant, 'followed by a fashion parade by twenty-four mannequins [models]… These lovely young ladies will parade in Australian sports clothes, and demonstrate the famous Darling Folding Umbrellas.' There would be dancing after the display, presumably without umbrellas.

In the final matches of the tour Harry was given the opportunity to fulfil his wish of playing up front, turning out at centre-forward and scoring twice against Granville District at the Cumberland Oval, Paramatta, on 18 July, a game rescheduled from June because of incessant rain. Granville were no pushovers, with four internationals in their ranks and there was no score at half time. After a talking to by Reg Flewin behind closed doors during the break, England upped their game and Birmingham's Smith scored immediately after the restart before Harry made it two. He also headed in a Langton corner at the close. Wiseman once again did his bit to further cordial relations between England and Australia by observing: 'We've just about had this tour. We're tired.' Six players, including Harry, with a badly bruised thigh, were being treated for injuries to get them ready for the Fifth and final test in Newcastle, New South Wales. Restored to his customary right back position, Harry, about whom the match programme commented, 'No greater back has toured this country than Bristol Rovers' Harry Bamford', helped England win 5-0 after a 'slight stir' before kick-off when England's other joint manager Frank Adams rejected the Australian ball provided because of its weight and size.

The final game of the tour, in which the English team recorded its 20th consecutive win on Australian soil was on the following day at Wollogong, where New South Wales were beaten 2-0, with Harry once again at centre-forward. He got the first goal after six minutes. The English had scored 153 goals, conceding 14, breaking playing as well as attendance records. Financially it was rated a huge success: 255,000 people paid £45,000 'to be dazzled by Soccer of a type never seen in Australia before'. The tour was estimated to have cost the Australian FA £36,000. But one newpaper complained that there had been too much emphasis on profit at the expense of giving new life to Australian soccer, which had been the stated aim of the tour. After the final test match, the Australian players were given £3 each in notes as their match fee.

Harry's England cap

Harry proudly wearing his cap back in Bristol

Well deserved R & R on the beach in Honolulu

A weary and bruised squad are given a
traditional greeting in Honolulu

After a farewell dinner in Newcastle, where each member of the England team was presented with a gold wristlet watch by the Australian FA, the weary tour party set off for home, where the new football season would be starting in two weeks. Harry kept his itinerary from British Commonwealth Pacific Airlines which reveals there had been a considerable rethink of the return trip. Originally, the party would have had a tortuous route back with five flights in three days, two of those internal flights in Canada. Now they would be flying to Fiji, where showers, refreshments and an evening meal awaited them at the Mocambo hotel, before an overnight flight to Honolulu (on which the players had beds). In Honolulu, 'Hula girls – island tour' and a hotel meal had been provided, before they flew to San Francisco and on to New York and an overnight stay in the Hotel Paramount before an afternoon flight on 27 July to London. Why there was such a big change we can only surmise, but it was certainly welcomed by the players. Harry had a camera and took some photographs of the trip – and there are snaps of him and his team mates, lei flower garlands around their necks, sunning themselves on a Honolulu beach with their trousers rolled up. The return journey did not go entirely smoothly; the aircraft developed engine trouble some distance out of New York but could not fly back there because of thunderstorms, so was re-routed to Boston for eight hours while one of engines was changed. This didn't fix the problem and the plane was diverted to Shannon airport where they had another five hour wait.

Harry had fifty dollars saved to spend and the papers reported that he had spent it on six nylon shirts. Younger readers will be unimpressed by this purchase, but those longer in the tooth will remember how nylon shirts were considered a miraculous deliverance from the problems of washing, drying and ironing heavy cotton ones in the days before tumble driers and steam irons. Publicly, Harry had nothing but good things to say about the trip. 'Fit after nearly three months of steak, eggs, cream, ham, fruit and salad, he commented: "It was a first-rate trip. We were treated with the utmost hospitality. I only hope the Australian FA learned something from us."' He was less complimentary about

Happy to be going home

Australian football: 'They are not up to our standard. This is because I feel there is too little football played in the schools and because most of the players are amateurs. But there is interest in the game out there – a crowd of 43,000 attended the first match.'

On his first full day back Harry went to Eastville where he was featured showing a picture of the cricket ground where the first Test took place (a picture which still survives in the family papers) to Geoff Bradford and Bert Tann. But there would be little time for him to dwell on the tour – or recover from it, as the new season was about to begin.

CHAPTER 7

'Far Below the Incomparable Harry of Last Season'

'A familiar figure strolled into Eastville Stadium today with a British Overseas Airways Corporation satchel over his shoulder. It was round-the-world-in-three-months 'Digger' Bamford… not nearly as brown as those who stayed at home, and he has not cultivated an Australian accent or returned with a bush hat.' This is how Peter Barnes, reporter for the *Evening World*, announced Harry's return to work after his triumphant Australian tour. Bert Tann graciously awarded him three days holiday before he resumed training.

Harry had, he himself said, come back injury-free and stimulated by playing alongside top-class players. He told Barnes: 'It was just what the doctor ordered. You know, you find yourself playing better the higher you go, it seems easier.' The incidents which had caused such a furore in the Australian papers were, according to Harry, exaggerated. He had been unaware, for example, that there was any glass on the pitch until the groundsman had shown him half a bucket full of the fragments which had been picked up.

After playing on 8 August 1951 in a cricket game for Rovers against Knowle, which the footballers won, Harry took part in the annual Rovers' trial game at Frenchay Cricket Ground watched by 300 die-hard spectators in driving rain. During the close season, the Eastville pitch had been raised 14 inches on a layer of cinders and the turf relaid. The players declared themselves happy with the lush grass, but for the time being it had to be allowed to bed in, hence the shift to Frenchay. This game was to have considerable consequences for both Harry and the Rovers' team, because during it he collided with Bill Roost and

Harry's Rovers' blazer badge

sustained knocks to his knee and ankle which left him unable to come out for the second half. The knee injury quickly responded to treatment in the gleaming new Rovers' treatment room which had been paid for by the supporters' club. But the ankle did not improve and was very swollen. It became clear that there would be the unusual sight of a Rovers' team without Harry Bamford lining up for the first match against Walsall away. An out of sorts Rovers lost 1-0; Harry's replacement, his old full-back partner Barry Watkins, was highly experienced and played 'a solid game'. But the *Evening World* lamented that when Harry was not on the pitch, not only did Rovers' defence suffer, but also their forward play: 'The old understanding there used to be between Bamford and Pitt was missing, and this was an important factor in the game.'

The injury proved stubborn. The collision with Roost could have happened at any time, but it is not unlikely that the enormous amount of football Harry had played beforehand had something to do with its severity and slow healing. When he arrived at Eastville on 30 July he had been playing football continuously for 11 months; between 19 August 1950 and 22 July 1951, Harry had played 74 competitive games: 45 in the League, 11 in the cup and 18 on tour. None of the England party Down Under played more. Many of these were high pressure matches for a team chasing promotion and on a record-breaking FA cup run, or on the bone-hard Australian pitches which the professionals hated. Although Geoff Bradford went on the FA tour to the West Indies in 1955 and George Petherbridge was selected to tour South Africa the following year, these tours were shorter and both made far fewer appearances than Harry.

In Rovers' next game, a home tie against Swindon Town which they won 1-0 in front of the second highest gate ever at Eastville, the biggest concern was not Harry's absence, but the new pitch which 'played all sorts of tricks'. The bounce was unpredictable, the ball swerving unexpectedly. Jackie Pitt put on a lacklustre performance and the papers speculated that he was missing Harry. Left-half Peter Sampson later described how this partnership worked. "All the fiddly stuff – short passes of six or seven yards – was played down the right side of the field by Harry Bamford, Jackie Pitt and Georgie Petherbridge. Down the left, I linked up with full-back Geoff Fox and Josser Watling and we were very different players… So we didn't bother with the fancy footwork.' The left wing trio preferred to deliver an (accurate) long ball forward, in contrast to the complex interplay of those on the right. Sampson reminisced in the same interview that there were occasions when he'd 'go mad' with Harry over a defensive error, but Harry would just 'trot over, put his arm around my shoulder and say quietly, "Peter, please don't talk like that"'.

The new pitch continued to cause problems; the grass was too long but it couldn't be cut because it would affect the new turf bedding in and it slowed up Rovers' normal fast game. Shrewsbury Town snatched a late equaliser on 25 August to make the score 3-3, but Rovers rallied over the next three matches, scoring nine goals and conceding only one in two of those, 5-1 and 4-0 wins over Aldershot and Crystal Palace respectively. Their first home defeat of the season, still without Harry, was by a solitary goal on the 8 September against Watford.

Harry's first game back saw Rovers return to winning form in the return match against Crystal Palace on 12 September at Selhurst Park which they won 1-0. Worryingly, he broke down in the second half and limped for the rest of the game. At Ashton Gate on 15 September in the first Bristol derby of the season, a 1-1 draw, the same thing happened again. He kicked the ball hard, his ankle became sore and once again he limped off the field. Peter Barnes in the *Evening World* observed that Harry was obviously not back to his old level, but that 'his return has been the means of bringing Jackie Pitt back to his true form'. Rumours began to spread about the severity of the injury and the *Evening World* found it necessary to scotch stories that Harry's football career was finished. The ankle, it reported, had been subjected to a variety of treatments – heat ray and electrical massage among them. But there were still 'lesions' left. These lesions, it had been advised, could be loosened only by strenuous practice and match play, so that Bert Tann's only option had been to return Harry to the first team 'where his absence was so badly felt, which he did, knowing full well that an awkward kick or a sudden jolt of the ankle might temporarily break down the old injury'. The injury was improving week by week and Harry had felt no after effects after his two games and the ankle had not swollen up. In the derby he continued to so 'some fine work in the old Bamford style' right to the end of the game, despite clearly being in some discomfort. Probably Harry was suffering from an osteochondral lesion in his ankle, the modern treatment for which would be surgery or rest, not playing a hard 90 minutes.

Rovers had not had a bad start, but neither had they displayed the sparkling form of last season. However, there was frustration because this season's competition was deemed wide open and none of the teams fancied for promotion had shown any consistency. After 11 games, by the end of September when Rovers drew at home with Norwich, only seven points divided the 21 teams in Division Three South and Rovers were well placed in fourth. October and most of November were relatively barren months for the team, part of which was down to Harry's continual struggles to regain fitness. On 6 October at Eastville, with 20 minutes left to play against Northampton Town, Rovers were two goals adrift, both coming from bad defensive mistakes – not from Harry – but, according to the *Evening World*'s Pat Kavanagh, from an overworked Fox and Warren who were covering for a 'Bamford, still far below the incomparable Harry of last season'. Rovers failed to register a win in the seven matches between 29 September and 16 November, losing three times. One of those defeats was inflicted by Reading on 13 October in a game where both Bert Hoyle and Harry had 'a poor day'. Whenever Bainbridge, the opposing winger got the ball, 'Bamford seemed to be giving him 10 yards or more in which to work'. Other injuries also took their toll of the small Rovers' squad. Watling was ordered to rest a bad knee for a few weeks and even Bert Tann was confined to bed with a heavy cold.

Tann missed the Rovers' visit to Southend on 27 October and avoided having to witness them losing 2-1. Also absent were Hoyle and Harry, who had been dropped to the Reserves and were playing against West Ham in the Football Combination back at Eastville, alongside Bill Roost who had become unsettled after offers from other clubs. The Reserves were a goal down until the referee introduced a white ball because of the bad light and Maurice Lockier, one of Harry's fruit-picking mates, promptly equalised with it. Hoyle had played 71 consecutive games for Rovers since signing from Exeter City until his replacement by the 21 year old Howard Radford, while Watkins once again stood in for Harry in the first team. There was no revival of Rovers' form in the following game, Bournemouth beating them 2-1, but Hoyle and Bamford helped the Reserves enjoy a 5-0 stroll against Luton.

Bert Tann didn't try dropping Harry again for the rest of the season, reverting to the tried and tested line up. Although the first team drew against Millwall on 10 November, Harry's brief stint in the Reserves appeared to have done him good and 'the Harry of old was back... sound, quicker in recovery and surer in kicking' as Rovers' played their best football of the season. The improvement continued in a 5-0 rout of Brighton at Eastville. As the cartoonist Speed in the *Evening World* remarked: 'Rovers fielded their old cup side and – what is more important – they fielded their old cup field and ere ninety minutes had elapsed, the Eastville quicksands had claimed yet another victim'. The pitch re-laying had not been a success and Rovers, quickly adapting to the all too familiar conditions, played open football. Their opponents kept them out until 40 seconds before the interval, when Rovers won a penalty smashed home by Warren. Then, five minutes after the restart, Harry went to work. He came through with the ball from defence, hitting a perfectly placed centre for Bradford to increase the lead. The papers laid the credit for Rovers' upsurge firmly at Harry's educated feet: the *Sunday Dispatch* remarked that his return to form 'has given confidence to the whole defence' and that spearheading many of the attacks with Petherbridge, Harry had a hand in all of Rovers' four second half goals.

The *Evening* World bemoaned the consequences of his injury for Harry's chances of winning a full England cap: 'With the present scarcity of top-class right backs, his form of last season may have got him among the players who will be reporting at Manchester tomorrow [for an England squad meeting]. Bamford is a better bet than [Bert] Mozley of Derby, when in the mood.' In an article celebrating the honour of the hanging of a photograph of Harry in his blue and silver England B cap on the Eastville boardroom wall alongside that of Irish international Matt Mahoney, a predecessor of Warren, the paper analysed in detail exactly what '"Big Harry" as he is known to Eastville 'Erb' contributed to the team. Acknowledging that Harry had completely lost his touch, 'but he kept pegging away, refusing to be disheartened or disillusioned', it argued that Rovers now possibly had the strongest right flank in the Third Division, Petherbridge brilliant once he received the right sort of service from Bamford and Pitt, and Roost, now at inside right, receiving more and better passes and freed from having to chase the ball constantly. 'And Bamford is the man who by sheer football ability has welded the other three into a combination dreaded by opposing defences.' The article quoted this tribute from Ted Vizard, when he was Wolves' manager: 'Harry Bamford is the best inside-forward I have ever seen playing full-back and in my team I wouldn't play him anywhere else but full-back. If a team has one full back who is a stopper and one who can play Bamford's sort of game successfully it can't go far wrong.'

17 games of the season were over before Harry was back to his best – five of those were defeats, but seven were draws, and as wins were worth two points only Rovers were not yet without hope of promotion. The start of another FA Cup competition also led to optimism that there would be another storming campaign. The draw had paired Rovers with Kettering Town from the Southern Football League. On paper, the tie looked easy, but the Poppies had a team laced with experience, including goalkeeper Pickering who had the reputation of being the longest kicker of a dead ball of all the keepers in the country. Rovers fielded their old

giant-killing cup line up – 'It's That Team Again' said the *Evening World* – and, after a night of torrential rain which left pools of water on the deteriorating Eastville surface, Rovers blew away their opposition in a devastating 15 minute spell: 'Bamford, apart from keeping Joyner under control, indulged in a couple of typical runs which had the Kettering defence dizzy'. Rovers followed up with a second consecutive 5-0 victory, against Torquay United in the League, Petherbridge putting on a brilliant display to score four, although the Charlton manager Jimmy Seed who was in the crowd was most impressed by Harry's performance in defence, exclaiming afterwards to reporters: 'What a great back! He does the work of two men'.

The team had finally found some form, beating Ipswich away before their FA Cup tie against another team from the Southern League, Weymouth Town, known as the 'Terras' from one of the colours of their strip quartered in terracotta and blue. Weymouth had their own plan to force a draw and a replay at the Recreation Ground, manager and left-back Jack Taylor claiming to have spotted a 'small loophole' in Rover's 'defence in depth scheme': 'Bamford, with his lightning dribbles, is liable to produce a goal at any moment, but our boys will have orders to belt the ball back to the left wing – as soon as they can rob Harry, that is!' The Terras had little chance to test Taylor's theory, their players more preoccupied by wading through the mud and sand mixture of the Eastville pitch, and Rovers went through to the next round comfortably with goals from Lambden and Petherbridge.

Although Rovers lost their next League game 2-1 away at Shrewsbury, playing their cup team for the seventh match in a row, there were extenuating circumstances as an injury to Josser Watling reduced them to ten men for three-quarters of the match, and they went on to win two and draw one of the three remaining games of the year. Rovers began 1952 in seventh place, still promotion outsiders. The New Year also began with another two points after a convincing 3-0 away defeat of Watford. Walter Winterbottom, the England manager, was watching and he saw Harry being given the run around by Tony Collins, the Watford outside-left, for the first ten minutes. This prompted the opinion that

'Twinkletoes': Harry was a surprisingly dainty dribbler of the ball maybe he was a little stale after so much football in the past 18 months. But Harry soon got the measure of Collins whom he played out of the game. Winterbottom's final comment gave no clue as to any possible future England call up: 'He's still a very fine player'.

Along with their reviving hopes in the League, Rovers' fans had a glamour tie in the FA Cup to anticipate. Their opponents were First Division 'Proud' Preston North End. Disappointingly, Preston's superstar winger Tom Finney, one of the greatest English footballers ever, was injured and had to watch the game from the grandstand, but Preston were still a draw and cup fever returned to Eastville with a vengeance. Bert Tann once again took his team off to Southend where they sampled the delights of the English seaside, newspaper photographs showing them visiting a model of Drake's galleon *The Golden Hind*, the players posing precariously high up in the rigging. It did the trick; Rovers overturning the form book to win 2-0 in front of nearly 31,000, with Harry 'imperturbable' at right-back. Preston's manager Will Scott blamed the pitch, calling it 'atrocious – the worst ground we have played on in living memory. We could not play the kind of football we like.' But Bert Tann was having none of it: 'Preston are a great side and have many fine players. Surely first-class players should be able to adapt themselves to any conditions. Football is, after all, a winter game.'

Another two wins followed, including a 2-0 defeat of Bristol City, but Rovers' season would start to unravel at the end of January. They won only once in the next seven games. There was an exodus from Bristol to Southend for the next round of the FA Cup, the Deputy Lord Mayor of Bristol and the MP for Bristol South leaving the city along with thousands packed onto four official trains and 150 coaches. Despite a break, in Margate this time, and the team, ordered by the FA to wear all black socks which had been difficult to find and were finally bought from ex-Arsenal player Wally Barnes' sports shop in London, taking the lead through Geoff Bradford, Rovers' luck ran out. Bill Roost was carried off on a stretcher. The winning goal for Southend nine minutes from time was scored by Peter Sampson's cousin Les Stubbs. Rovers seem to have had a perfectly good goal disallowed, the ball hitting the upright and bouncing down– over the line, according to photographs in the Bristol papers.

A few days later on 6 February, King George VI died in his sleep at Sandringham and no football was to be played in London for five days while his body lay in state. After a miserable 1-0 defeat by Norwich City in the snow of Carrow Road, one reporter quoted a Norwich spectator as saying: 'What's the matter with them? They're not the Bristol Rovers of old.'

To fill up the empty cup weekend, a friendly was arranged with First Division Fulham on 23 February, the confrontation between Harry Bamford and Charlie Mitten, the 'Bogota Bandit', the English international winger who had sensationally left Manchester United to play in Colombia where there was no maximum wage, making the Bristol sports reporters lick their lips. 'The friendly... rapidly became a duel between two men... Dazzling ball control came from both players,' said one, 'but in the main I have never seen 'Big Harry' so completely beaten, Mitten pushed the ball around the outside and inside, between his legs and crossed the ball with consummate artistry.' Mitten's display, in the satin shorts favoured by Fulham which excited much comment, was even more remarkable given the conditions. Rovers' groundstaff were spending six days of the week trying to get the pitch into shape and the players were taken off training to join the 'Mud Battle', their feet actually disappearing into the ooze as they forked the ground to drain it. Bristol City even offered Rovers the chance to play their home games at Ashton Gate.

Unaffected by his roasting by Mitten, Harry continued to show his best form of the season, kicking off the goal line in several games. On 29 March, the then smallest post-war gate of 4,666 at Eastville was recorded, as heavy drifting snow, up to two feet high in some places, led to widespread postponement of games. The hardy souls who made it out (there were no ball boys or mascots) and endured the stormy conditions saw Rovers beat Millwall 2-1 with a goal from Bradford three minutes from the end.

While eventual Third Division South champions Plymouth Argyle won 17 of their last 18 games, Rovers were inconsistent. There were some high scoring victories. Both full-backs Harry and Geoff Fox made their 200th appearance for Rovers in a 5-0 rout of Gillingham. In the next match two days later, Rovers recorded their biggest win of the season, a six-nil defeat of Colchester, Vic Lambden bagged four goals and broke club and personal records in doing so. His goals, which came in 34 minutes, were his quickest hat-trick and also took his League total for the season to 29, three more than the club record set last season. Lambden also equalled the best individual score by a Rovers' man in a single match.

Injuries now began to take their toll. Against Torquay on 19 April, Tann was forced to play an unknown amateur centre-half, Stan Green, who had only been at the club a week after joining from a Birmingham works team. 'Rovers famous defensive system wobbled at Torquay today,' observed the *Evening World*, 'Bamford looked rather shaky'.

Harry missed the penultimate League game against Walsall because of a damaged thigh muscle. He was also missing from the Gloucestershire Senior Cup Final, which Rovers lost. It was announced more money would be spent on the pitch, fine flint gravel being laid under it to help drainage, work which began as soon as the last home game finished so that, unlike the previous summer, the new surface would have plenty of time to settle. Despite the disappointing end to the season, Rovers had scored 97 goals, the highest total in the club's history. Vic Lambden netted his 100th goal in post-war football on 26 April to give Rovers a victory over Ipswich. The signs were there that Rovers were a formidable team which, if it could avoid injuries, would, with Harry Bamford at his best and having a proper break from football in the summer, be able to mount a serious challenge for the Third Division South title.

CHAPTER 8

Crowning Glory

Despite the relatively downbeat finish to the previous term, Rovers' fans sensed that this might be their season. Season tickets were snapped up, 75% sold by the beginning of August 1952. The £6,000 earned contrasted sharply with the mere £620 sales had brought in five years before. Harry appeared in the papers in the summer presenting a troop shield for a competition at a Scout camp in Somerset, as well as some proficiency badges. Prophetically, he told the boys: 'To be successful in anything needs good team spirit'.

The Rovers would be training away from Eastville for 12 months on the Memorial Ground Annexe on Filton Avenue in Horfield, the home of Bishopston Rugby Club, while the new pitch bedded in. It was not going to need watering. August brought heavy floods to West Somerset, North Devon and Exmoor, the worst in living memory, leaving many houses in Bristol without electricity. On 20 August, Harry was one of the Rovers' team who travelled to Barnstaple for a benefit game which raised £350 for the picturesque village of Lynmouth, devastated when the West and East Lyn rivers broke their banks, destroying houses and killing more than 30 people. The Rovers took the game very seriously, winning 7-1, their 'dour' defence' allowing the home forwards few scoring opportunities.

The season where so much was expected began with a fortunate home win over Shrewsbury Town watched by one of the three biggest crowds in Division Three. At first, it appeared that the match might not go ahead, as the referee was nowhere to be found, and secretary John Gummow broadcast an appeal for a qualified referee to the crowd. The six men who immediately came forward must have been disappointed when the wayward official eventually showed up. Bert

Tann experimented with a new right flank of summer signings John McIlvenny and Paddy Leonard, moving George Petherbridge over to the left, but the pairing found it hard to adjust to the pace of the play and was barracked by jittery supporters for their slowness. With the score level at 1-1, Rovers were awarded a penalty in the 89th minute, which 'No Nerves Ray' Warren smashed home to delight fans in the ground, as well as those listening on the hospital radio system in seven Bristol hospitals. Rovers' director John Hare made Bristol sports history with the first ever running commentary in the city by direct line to the patients. The broadcast was so popular it became a regular feature, though the game's nailbiting denouement can't have done much good on the cardiac wards.

Disappointingly, Rovers lost their next game, the home side Torquay taking both points thanks to a 'tragic mistake' by keeper Bert Hoyle which left him pounding the ground theatrically with his fist. A routine back header from Warren spun out of his grasp and into the goal. Rovers, with a second new right flank pairing, McIlvenny and Leonard replaced by new signing Desmond Jones and Andy Micklewright, were not at their best and kept making mistakes, although the *Evening Post*'s Traveller exempted Harry from criticism, describing him as 'solid as Gibraltar. He intercepted passes laid on for his opponents with as little flurry as if he were tending pigeons in his own backyard. His distribution of the ball and his prompting of an indifferent attack were alike excellent.'

Harry was once again at the top of his game in the next match, a 5-3 victory over Brough Fletcher's Walsall. Pat Kavanagh in the *Evening World* joined the chorus of those celebrating Harry's return to the form of the season before last: 'This was a Bamford who positioned himself brilliantly and who returned to those long, accurate passes, which turned defence into attack in a trice'. But the newspapers were not getting carried away, preaching caution about Rovers' title chances. Walsall were one of the League's weakest sides and had it not been for Harry and his 'thoughtful piece of footcraft' in which he 'never put a foot wrong' they might have scored more. There was speculation about how the veterans in the Rovers' team, among whom Harry, who would turn 32 in October, was included, along with his partner on the right Jackie Pitt, also 32 and elder statesman Ray Warren, 34, would cope with the gruelling campaign which lay ahead. The players listed gave their own answer. All three were ever present in the League and the FA Cup, 50 games all told; Peter Sampson, Geoff Fox and Vic Lambden also played every League game and Geoff Bradford missed only the last League game of the season.

On 6 September, Rovers went second in the table after beating Gillingham 3-1 at Eastville, Harry having a 'great game, both in defence – when he coolly broke up many dangerous Gillingham raids – and in setting his own forward line in motion with those well-known long raking upfield passes which found right winger Jones with unerring accuracy'. When Rovers beat Colchester away in the next match, a queue forming outside the *Evening World* offices of folk desperate to know the score, they went top for the first time in two years. The papers began showing the top of the Division Three South table at the start of match reports, a stylised hand pointing to Rovers perched at the top of the tree. Bert Tann took his team to a show in London's West End to celebrate the two points. Rovers were staying in the capital for their next game against Millwall, and arrived at the ground with a police escort, which was nothing to do with the famous ferocity of the Lions' fans, but because their coach driver lost his way in Bermondsey and a patrol car he asked for directions offered to guide them through the busy streets. Two Millwall goals in five minutes put a dent in Rovers' title charge, followed by a Fox own goal four minutes from time.

In the return against Colchester back at Eastville, Harry showed that he might have made a good goalkeeper. Unfortunately, as Bert Hoyle was also on the pitch, his save gave away a penalty. Hoyle had only partly cleared a cross from the right and Harry made a flying leap across goal to push out a shot from John McKim. Hoyle nearly saved the spot kick, but it slipped through his hands and his legs into the net. Rovers still won 3-1. After a goalless stalemate in the first Bristol derby of the season, Dally Duncan, Luton's manager came to watch Rovers' 3-2 away victory against Watford and confirmed that he would like to 'talk business' if Rovers ever thought of letting Bamford leave, 'for Mr. Duncan hasn't forgotten a certain cup game two seasons ago'. Despite another goalless draw against Exeter, Rovers still occupied top spot, a point ahead of Norwich City, whom they beat in the final game of a packed September to establish a three point gap. There was discussion that 'no buy, no sell' should be abandoned to ensure that promotion didn't slip out of Rovers' grasp once again, but the policy did mean that Rovers could hang on to their best players – Bill Roost, for example, was about to return to the first team after Tann had resolutely refused to let him go.

Promotion fever had well and truly hit Eastville. 1,000 rattle-waving supporters travelled to Coventry on 4 October filling 16 coaches, a record for a Rovers' away game, and jammed into the away enclosure to see a 1-1 draw. With a quarter of the season gone, Rovers were two points ahead of Northampton, but four of their next six matches were away from home. The first of these away games was against their nearest challengers. In injury time, Northampton were winning 2-0. With a lively and aggressive attack, the Cobblers were a real handful, especially as Warren was in considerable pain from a groin injury for 80 minutes, and could have scored five or six goals, but they 'did not do so principally because that consistently good full-back Harry Bamford was at his very best'. What happened next could be seen in retrospect as a crucial moment in the season. Bryan Bush on the left-wing took a surprise shot which beat the goalie and Geoff Bradford followed it up with a header from a Petherbridge centre to give Rovers the draw and demonstrate their 'Merchant Venturers' spirit'. Bert Tann put the grandstanding finish down to his training methods. Not a believer in the 'too-strenuous training system', he wanted his players to 'keep all their strength for Saturday and not leave it on the training ground'. Hence the Rovers 'slaved' for a month pre-season, then were kept fit by playing two matches a week. A 12 match unbroken run followed. On 25 October, promotion rivals Ipswich were blown away 5-1, with four goals in the second half. Although they were unbeaten on their new pitch, Rovers were playing better away from Eastville, which Tann put down to having to adjust to a good surface!

With what might be seen at best as staggeringly bad timing and at worst a complete disregard for what the Rovers' revival was doing for the city, the Corporation's Bristol Development Plan proposed that an 80ft motor road out of the city be built at Eastville – cutting away part of the stadium terracing and passing within ten feet of the greyhound track. When the team were attracting the biggest crowds in their history, these proposals would cut capacity by 5,000-7,000 according to John Hare the general manager of Bristol Greyhound Racing Association, who spoke against them at the public enquiry, although the Corporation disputed his figures, claiming the reduction would be closer to 3,000. As Hare told the meeting, Rovers were 'expecting big things'. Speed gave the plans the lampooning they deserved in a cartoon showing a Rovers' forward skilfully dribbling round a lamp post to score – in off a Belisha beacon.

Despite ongoing heavy rain, the new pitch had no standing water on it when November began with the visit of Reading. Lambden put the home team ahead in the ninth minute and Rovers were 4-0 up within the first half hour. Reading's two wingers were completely shut out by Harry and Geoff Fox. 'Outside-right [Dennis] Simpson was Reading's best forward. But look who he had to beat – Bamford, playing wonderfully well', said one report. Reading's satin shorts ('the finest combination of silk pants that we've seen in post-war soccer, not even Fulham managed this') caused much comment, Bob Bennett's cartoon in the *Evening Post* suggesting that: 'Harry Bamford gets a pair with a shirt to match to add the finishing touch to his terpsichorean gyrations along the touch line'. Traveller repeated a comment made to him by a Reading supporter: 'I make Bamford the best right-back in the Southern section'. Not that everyone was pleased by the 4-0 victory. Pat Kavanagh opined that Rovers should not have eased up and scored more in the second half as their goal average was not as good as Norwich's.

Rovers' supporters club enrolled its 8,000 member, Gordon Hazell, an up and coming Bristol middleweight boxer who was training for a fight with the French champion (which he won) and large numbers of

Bob Bennett suggests a change to Harry's kit

those fans went to Bournemouth on 8 November, along with chairman Hampden Alpass. He had lifted his attendance ban at away matches, self-imposed since he had gone to Torquay to watch Rovers lose at the end of August – the sixth away defeat in a row he had witnessed. The other directors persuaded him to go – and the 'hoodoo' was lifted, Rovers winning a tight game 2-1. 'If they'd lost I don't think I would ever have gone away with Rovers again', the relieved chairman admitted afterwards.

The winning run in the League went on, but the arrival of the first round of the FA Cup provoked a debate which would be all too familiar to modern football supporters. Rovers drew Leyton Orient away, the first time for three years they would meet a League side in the opening game. The suggestion was aired that it would be a good thing if Bristol Rovers were to make an early exit from the competition, as no team in recent seasons had come close to winning any League title while having a good cup run. The 'double' of League and Cup had last been won in 1897. The discussion intensified when Rovers had to replay the drawn tie two days later on 24 November, on a freezing afternoon beset by snowstorms – later that night the city docks froze over – in front of 15,032. The papers described this relatively low turnout as 'an unofficial boycott… by supporters who apparently had the mistaken idea that it would be a good scheme for their team to be beaten in the first round.' Given that the attendance at the next game, against Brighton on 29 November, again played in such a heavy snowstorm that half a dozen men with brooms were kept busy clearing the touchlines while the game was in progress, was 11,647, avoidance of hypothermia rather than a boycott seems a better explanation. The stay-at-homes missed a terrific performance and the Rovers' then highest League score ever. 'Every Rovers man was at the top of his game', enthused the *Pink 'Un*, including Harry Bamford, 'who played a stirring game'. The 7-0 scoreline could have been bigger. Bradford had a goal disallowed 'for reasons no one could understand, the referee saying that Bradford had intended to foul the goalkeeper and the fact that he headed the ball into the net was incidental'.

Those who genuinely wanted to see the Rovers out of the Cup would have been disappointed on 6 December when they beat Midland League team Peterborough by a single Vic Lambden goal to go into the Third Round where they would meet Second Division Huddersfield Town who in their last 20 matches had conceded only 12 goals. Meanwhile, in the League Rovers marched on through the rest of December, unbeaten since 13 September and stretching their lead to five points after victories over Crystal Palace and Shrewsbury Town. Shrewsbury turned out to be tough opponents who threw everything at Rovers after Bush gave them the lead shortly after the break. Fox kicked off the line to save a certain goal after Harry, Warren and Hoyle were all beaten; another time three Rovers' defenders missed the ball before Harry put it into touch. Their next opponents were equally tough; despite being reduced to ten men for most of the game Queens Park Rangers attacked the Rovers' rearguard ferociously. 'And here were Harry Bamford and Geoff Fox holding the Rovers fort like the good old defenders they are'. Harry was deemed man of the match for his efforts and the 2-1 win set a Rovers' record of 20 games without defeat – and, more importantly – gave them a seven point cushion. Rovers were the only team in all Leagues to score 40 points before the turn of the year, dropping only eight points in their 24 matches.

Rovers were not the only team in Bristol prospering. The City were also putting in a surge and the papers speculated that more soccer history could be made if the Robins won their next league game, with Bristol clubs first and second in the Division Three South table for the first time. Rovers had their away cup tie against in form Huddersfield to negotiate on 10 January 1953. Tann took them to a panto, *Cinderella*, the night before, but also announced that if Rovers were eliminated the team would go to Bognor for a week's holiday. 4,000 Rovers' fans went north, among them 'Pa' Wookey of Stapleton Road, Rovers' oldest fan, Bristol Telephone Exchange reporting a mass booking of 4.30am alarm calls so that the early trains from Temple Meads wouldn't be missed. Huddersfield proved to be too strong, scoring twice without reply. Neither Fox nor Harry had a particularly good game and Bert Tann, observing that this was 'not the real Bristol Rovers' suggested that the cup exit was 'a blessing in disguise. There will be no split objectives now, and we can really go after the League'. Bristol City also lost their chance of going into second place with a draw – the historic moment was going to have to wait – until 24 January.

The five months of abnormal cold and extreme weather which had prevailed since September showed no signs of abating. Rovers had taken matters into their own hands in December, deciding not to wait for the Corporation to do anything about potential flooding from the Frome. As a temporary defence, a two-foot concrete retaining wall was constructed which it was hoped would last 15 years and prevent the river sabotaging the promotion push. It was a wise move. On 31 January, Harry shone again in Rovers' 4-1 home win against Aldershot in the trickiest of conditions. A howling high wind played 'many strange tricks with the ball, which often curled in the wrong direction'. Traveller in the *Post* awarded Harry 'full marks' for subduing the ex-Spurs winger Ken Flint and 'with a clever dribble' often going up field 'to bang in a shot'. The *Evening World*'s Pat Kavanagh was equally complimentary, but not so enamoured of Harry's cavalier style: 'His forays upfield occasionally left Pitt trying to stop two or three men'. The high wind which disrupted the football was an ominous forerunner of worse to come. That night a tsunami-like tidal surge in the North Sea brought death to hundreds along the coasts of East Anglia, Essex, Kent and the Netherlands, as well as sinking the car ferry Princess Victoria which was headed for Larne in Northern Ireland, with the loss of 133 lives.

A crowd of 40,000 was expected at Ashton Gate for the season's second Bristol derby on 7 February, white lines having been painted leading to the turnstiles. People queued for five hours. Inside the ground, entertainment was provided in the form of a coffee trolley and community singing, songsheets with the words of popular songs adapted for the occasion distributed. 'Widecombe Fair' became: 'To the Rovers, the Rovers the team of the year, Upalong, upalong, out of the Third. Your record is good, the best that we've heard, With Harry Bamford etc. etc. ... and Uncle Bert Tann and all'. The keenly awaited 'Battle of Bristol', perhaps predictably, ended in a goalless draw. David Jack was particularly impressed by Rovers' defence, unchanged for 29 games, which 'continued to display that particular brand of cool, attractive football so much a feature of the Rovers' success, and no player contributed more than right back Harry Bamford, who, shunning the hasty clearance, repeatedly stroked the ball gently to a waiting colleague'.

The dreadful weather claimed one more casualty, which could have spelt disaster for Rovers' prospects. Bert Hoyle, the Rovers' highly popular goalkeeper, regularly presented with oranges by fans, the juice of which he had become accustomed to use to keep his palms sticky while playing in goal when he was serving as a commando in the desert, was the only Rovers' player allowed to live far away from Bristol in his hotel, the Ship Inn in Dawlish. Hoyle estimated that he travelled 570 miles a week when Rovers were at home, 700 miles plus when they were away. After the derby, Ken Powell, Rovers' young reserve centre-half, was driving Hoyle back to Dawlish in his open tourer car when the car skidded and overturned onto the grass verge. Hoyle was catapulted through the canvas roof and landed 18 feet away; Powell was pinned behind the steering wheel. Both lay there in the darkness for some time, until the upturned car was spotted by the Mayor of Glastonbury, who tracked them down from Powell's loud groans. Both were rushed to the Bristol Royal Infirmary, where Hoyle was found to have a skull fracture and his condition was said to be 'serious'.

Even before Hoyle's accident, Rovers had drawn their last two home games, and, as young Howard Radford stepped into Hoyle's very big shoes, their promotion charge began to slow down and it was up to the senior men to dig deep. On 14 February, they met Exeter on their snow-covered pitch which by the end of the game had become a 'slushy morass' on which the ball 'skidded crazily,... for a while, as players miskicked and slipped, it looked as if the game would develop into a parody of a pantomime on ice'. In the circumstances, an away draw was a good result, as Exeter had not been beaten by any of the top teams in the Division. The *Evening Post* gave the credit to two men: 'The Rovers were indebted to Bamford and Pitt in defence. The former started shakily but gradually found his feet and ended by being outstanding'. The statistics bore out how much the Rovers had their defence to thank for keeping them at the top of the table for five months. Rovers were unbeaten in 23 League matches and conceded only 14 goals. As the news came through that Hoyle was off the danger list, Bert Tann, reluctant to panic buy, asked neighbours City to help with his goalkeeping crisis by loaning out their reserve keeper Con Sullivan, but Pat Beasley felt unable to oblige saying that Sullivan was injured. Then City put a price tag of £5,000 on Sullivan which sent Tann on a frantic tour to find another keeper he could sign before the deadline of 14 March. City did, however, do one 'good neighbour' act by beating Rovers' challengers Northampton Town on 23 February. The signing from Crystal Palace two days before the deadline for £2,000 of Bob Anderson, another ex-commando, as reserve keeper was the first proper transfer fee Rovers had paid for 14 years.

14 March was the day 'They Went Just Wild About Harry' – a 3-0 win over Ipswich at Eastville the occasion for Harry's goal for the season. Rovers were already two up when, ten minutes from the end, after he

DEFENDERS TOOK HONOURS IN ROVERS' SIXTH DOUBLE

By THE TRAVELLER

BRISTOL ROVERS, 3; IPSWICH TOWN, 0.

DEFEATING Ipswich Town, Bristol Rovers completed their sixth double of the present season and made their points total 55, equalling their best-ever record in the Southern Section, set up in season 1950-51.

With 23 wins, the Rovers have already beaten their previous best (20), achieved in seasons 1933-34 and the last two seasons.

The Rovers have been at the top of the League table exactly six months—since September 15, and they have another 12 matches to play.

Saturday's success was the Rovers' fourth consecutive victory over Ipswich and their ninth in 11 League games over the East Anglian side.

Although not giving one of their best displays of the season, the Rovers were well deserving of their win which, with the chances they had, should have been even more pronounced. In stating this, I do not, however, wish to discount the brilliant display of David Parry, the Ipswich goalkeeper, whose work must have impressed Mr. F. E. Morgan, the vice-president of the Welsh F.A., who was sitting in the stand.

Parry, who was "capped" for Wales against Scotland in 1951, made some wonderfully good clearances and crowned a great afternoon's work by stopping Warren's penalty kick.

FOUGHT BACK

When Petherbridge put the Rovers ahead in the third minute the spectators must have thought they were going to see a crop of goals. Ipswich, however, fought back quite well, but despite the good work done by the visiting defence the Rovers should have crossed over with a comfortable lead.

As it was, the Rovers did not increase their lead until the 69th minute, but Bradford's goal was well worth waiting for. It was a shot "from the blue" which would have beaten any goalkeeper.

It was Bradford's 26th goal of the season, so with Bristol City's Rodgers he is now joint leading scorer of the Southern Section with a goal more than Garneys, the Ipswich centre-forward.

Bamford's goal will long be remembered. It was a just reward for persistence and "guts." Even after his first shot had been stopped, and colliding with goalkeeper Parry he recovered the ball and banged it into the net.

It was not Bradford's first goal for the Rovers as a right-back. Playing in that position he scored their only goal against Newport County at Somerton Park on September 3 1951.

When playing for the Rovers in the forward line in season 1945-46—at inside-right, centre-forward, and inside-left—Bamford scored four goals. These facts may settle a number of arguments.

Petherbridge struck his best form.

He was fast and clever, easily beat his opponents, and sent over some perfect centres.

The whole Rovers' left-flank did well. Fox did better than in the previous home game, there was no better wing-half than Sampson, and Bradford played his usual forceful game.

Lambden was always a trier, but the ball did not run too kindly for him. I thought that, on the whole, Leonard pleased, but he was not as thrustful or really as quick as Bush. Leonard's footwork was clever—he sent out some nice passes —but he was not always sure whether to shoot or pass.

Ipswich were unfortunate when, 11 minutes from the end, their centre-half Rees, owing to a leg injury, had to leave the field. The match, however, was then won—and lost!

The attendance—21,244—was disappointing, nearly 3,000 fewer than watched the game with Walsall, the bottom team in the League, in January. Surely, with such a wonderful playing record the Rovers home matches should attract crowds between 25,000 and 30,000.

FULL-BACK HARRY BAMFORD about to score Rovers' third goal from a rebound, after his first shot had been stopped by goalkeeper Parry.

The Evening Post celebrates yet another Rovers' win and a sizzler of a goal from Harry

had put in another fine defensive display, Harry made absolutely sure of the victory with a fine solo effort. Picking up the ball well inside his own half, he ran the length of the field into the opposing penalty area, going past several players before tricking Deacon, the most experienced Ipswich defender, into moving the wrong way before he shot. His powerful strike hit goalkeeper Parry and as it rebounded he followed it up, colliding with the keeper, to hit it into the net. A standing ovation, in which the Ipswich players joined, greeted the goal. The cartoonists were much inspired by Harry's achievement. Bob Bennett caught the mood best by pointing out that after 27 League matches everyone was beginning to take a Rovers' victory for granted and the crowd was becoming blasé. But 'what sent us off home as though we'd swallowed a can of branded petrol? Why – our Harry's unconventional goal. Because you see, Harry's a back, now, and he isn't supposed to do things like that'. Harry, naturally drawn with a pair of pigeon's wings, was shown hanging his head in shame as Ray Warren told him he was ashamed of him, as he himself turned down the opportunity to score when he had the chance (Warren had missed a penalty). Speed focused on Harry's characteristic 'poker face', but couldn't resist a pigeon reference: 'Usually reliable sources report that Mr Bamford beat his men before scoring – but there is no truth in the story that a flight of racing pigeons hovered overhead – with football boots on. An official said that Mr Bamford was in considerable danger of breaking into a low, dry laugh – only iron control saved him!' Rovers' 55 points equalled their best ever record in the Southern section in 1950-51.

The next game, away against Reading on 21 March, put an end to the unbeaten run, Rovers conceding twice without reply. Harry was excellent, signalled out for praise in a tired performance, especially by the attack. John Coe in the *Evening Post* remarked: 'I shall not readily forget Bamford's deadly tackling and the non-stop stream of precision passes he laid on for his forwards, some of which really should have been better exploited than they were.' However, what seemed to be a combination of nerves and fatigue meant that Rovers made heavy work of crossing the finishing line. They won two out of their three Easter games, but went on to win only once in their last nine. Harry's form, so peerless for much of the season, nosedived along with that of the rest of the team. Against Swindon on 6 April, keeper Radford suffered a 20 minute blackout from concussion after being hit in the face by the ball, and Bob Anderson was drafted in to replace him. Against Newport County away on 13 April, Harry was unlucky to give away a penalty after colliding with the Newport forward Waite, and it set the seal on what for him was an uncharacteristically poor performance, one report commenting that he 'did not have a happy time' and that rarely had 'his

GOING UP.—Enthusiastic Rovers' fans invading the pitch to mob their heroes after the win over Newport.

Delirious Rovers' fans invade the pitch as Rovers' secure promotion with a win over Newport on 25 April 1953

judgement been so much at fault'. Tann turned to Bognor to provide the bracer his exhausted squad needed to make promotion certain, but the Rovers' stay was marred by a tragedy which cast a pall over everyone. Club director Lew Champeny, a very popular life-and-soul character, died in Salisbury hospital from injuries sustained in a car crash when he was driving back from visiting the team in their seaside retreat.

Home fans would, because of the quirks of the fixture list, have only one opportunity to see the Rovers at Eastville in their last five League games. This was Rovers' only victory, 3-1 over Newport County, with a hat-trick from Geoff Bradford. Promotion was now all but assured. The victory brought Rovers on to 63 points; chasers Northampton and Millwall could only achieve the same total if they won all of their last games and Northampton would have to win their final match by over 20 goals to overtake Rovers' superior goal average. Delirious spectators invaded the pitch at the end as their team went into Division Two for their first time in its history. Sadly, it was announced that Bert Hoyle would be forced to retire from the game following his head injury. The next game was something of an anti-climax, a 0-0 stalemate away at

BRISTOL ROVERS F.C. CHAMPIONS OF THIRD DIVISION (Southern Section) 1952 - 1953

Standing: Mr. J. Gummow (Secretary), Mr. B. Williams (Trainer), V. Lambden, J. Pitt, R. Anderson, G. Fox, B. Hoyle, H. Bamford, P. Sampson, His Grace The Duke of Beaufort (President).
Kneeling: G. Bradford, G. Petherbridge, R. Warren (Captain), W. Roost, J. Watling.
Inset left: Mr. H. J. Hampden Alpass (Chairman).   *Inset right:* Mr. B. Tann (Manager).

With the Compliments of the Bristol Brewery Georges & Co. Ltd.

A celebratory souvenir postcard from Georges' Brewery where Harry once worked

Each player was given a clock in thanks by the Supporters Club

Harry's magnificent Third Division (South) Championship winner's medal

Aldershot where the visitors played at half-pace and the Shots' left flank 'at times gave Harry Bamford his biggest run-around of the season'. Despite finishing with eight men in the forward line, Rovers couldn't find an equaliser in the League's closer, losing to Crystal Palace at Selhurst Park by a single goal in front of a tiny crowd of 5,629.

Rovers were to play a charity match against Cardiff City on the Badminton Estate of their President the Duke of Beaufort in aid of the National Playing Fields Association and it was decided that this would be the perfect opportunity for the Championship Shield to be presented in front of their fans. Over 11,000 made the trip there on Monday 4 May, sitting on hay bales and in carts, to see Rovers win 3-1. Harry was injured halfway through the first half and replaced by Bush, but can be seen in the newsreel shot by British Pathé running on to the pitch at the start. He wasn't fit enough to take part in the Gloucestershire Cup game, which Rovers lost 2-0, but he did have a beautiful, gold League winner's medal to add to his collection. The Bristol Rovers Supporters club also presented each member of the team with a small mantel clock with a commemorative inscription and Harry's is still in the family's possession.

Harry and Ray Warren in pre-season practice August 1953

Attention in Bristol now turned to the preparations for the Coronation in June. The centrepiece of the decorations was a giant crown, illuminated by 1,500 lights, which the papers marvelled would be as hot as thirty fires, to be lifted above the Centre gardens on a high platform. As part of the celebrations, a 'Queen of the Rovers' was also to be crowned. The winner, chosen by a panel which included up and coming young actress Joan Collins, 19 year old Barbara Pratten from Clifton, was selected for her 'deportment, charm, speaking voice and personality'. The prizes included a seat of honour at Rovers' matches throughout next season, a cake in the shape of a crown and a budgerigar in a cage. A pigeon may have been more appropriate.

CHAPTER 9

'Impeccable Harry'

'We can now reveal what Rovers are doing to set themselves for the Second League,' Speed's cartoon in the *Pink 'Un* on Saturday 30 May 1953 declared. 'The ground has been enlarged to accommodate 3,000 extra yelling fanatics; the mascot has been speeded up; Bill Roost is practising a courtesy campaign since it would never do to harass a second division goalkeeper and – they have evolved a special Everest rig out for their trips to the north next winter.' As for Harry Bamford – drawn rather unflatteringly with a tight-lipped, impassive, craggy face – he 'is practising a beautiful smile'.

When the Rovers players reported back for training on 24 July, both their full-backs were absent. Instead Harry and Geoff Fox were in Exeter, helping to coach young footballers from the National Federation of Boys' Clubs. Harry, who was 32, had been thinking hard about his future after football. In his personal papers there is an exercise book which shows that he attended some sort of book-keeping or accounts course. His daughter Hilary believes that this may have been because he was considering opening a sports shop when he retired. Hilary also remembers being told that he began to learn bricklaying, a trade which may have appealed because it would allow Harry, such a devotee of fresh air, to work outside, something which Josser Watling confirms in his Foreword with his story about them both working on Bert Tann's house. However, Tann, as we have seen, was a passionate advocate of coaching and encouraged his players to take the new training courses provided by the Football Association under the auspices of the England manager Walter Winterbottom which Tann himself had been one of the first former players to follow. Harry followed his manager's advice and took an elementary coaching course with the FA in the summer of this

Harry training by throwing a quoit with Bert Hoyle. Bill Roost is in the background

year. The next chapter will deal with Harry's training to become a coach in more detail.

Would the Rovers' team be able to cope with promotion to a higher League? George Baker in the *Evening World* reported how Bert Tann's 'Eastville system of coaching' had lifted many players 'from the ordinary to the talented' and that this summer they had all been provided with a special boot for training with a thick rubber sole with rubber studs and a string toe cap which was both good for kicking but also soft and easy to wear'. Tann's method was to work on fitness and ball skills. There was no mention of any tactical changes. Later, Geoff Fox, among others, admitted to the press that there was considerable apprehension in the dressing room about how Rovers would adjust. Unfortunately, the first two games of the season were away, Rovers' history-making first ever League match in the Second Division against tough opponents Fulham on 20 August, with Harry's old nemesis Charlie Mitten on the wing. The match had been rescheduled because building work on the home team's new stand was not yet completed and Rovers had protested unsuccessfully at having to play on that Thursday evening as they would be facing three matches in five days and travelling to both London and Blackburn.

Of this end-to-end humdinger, with eight goals, Pat Kavanagh commented: 'Craven Cottage is the name of Fulham's ground, but there was nothing craven about this game and no roses about the door of this cottage'. Rovers fielded the same side which won promotion: Anderson in goal; Bamford and Fox, Pitt, Warren and Sampson in defence; Petherbridge, Bradford, Lambden, Meyer and Watling in attack. They took the lead after 13 minutes through Geoff Bradford and had been more than holding their own when Fulham equalised on 38 minutes. Fox put Rovers ahead again at the start of the second half with a freak goal, putting in a high cross from the dead ball line which went over the goalkeeper's head into the net. Fulham came back – through that man Mitten – who made a 'dazzling run to beat Pitt and Bamford' before centring so accurately that future Newcastle, Barcelona and England manager Bobby Robson was able to head in his second from close range. Rovers took the lead for a third time in the 57th minute, Josser Watling's cross from the left wing hit goalwards by Petherbridge but parried, Bradford hooking in the rebound. Another Mitten cross set up Fulham's third equalizer. Then Robson had a hand – literally – in his third goal to put Fulham ahead, illegally pulling Mitten's centre down before shooting. It looked as if Rovers would have nothing to show for their efforts, until Josser Watling again raced down the wing and centred for Bradford to score the best goal of the game and rescue a point.

The overall verdict was that 'heroic' Rovers had shown they could 'make the higher grade football in one stride'. Clifford Webb (a Bristolian) wrote in the *Daily Herald*: 'I rate it quite a feat... I would say that what must have pleased Bert Tann more than anything was the absence of panic among his men'. Harry and Geoff Fox were singled out for praise by the local papers. 'The biggest Rovers' asset was the way their full backs Bamford and Fox cut out Mitten and [Arthur] Stevens, the Fulham wingers. It meant playing their defensive game more square than usual, but the way Bamford intercepted many passes intended for his international opponent, was lovely to watch.' Although, it has to be said, to modern eyes, praising the defence when it let in four goals and Harry in particular when Mitten got round him twice to create two of them, seems odd. It can probably be explained by the notion of 'individual duels' – that players faced a particular opponent and it was their job to subdue them. Harry obviously 'won' most of these with Mitten in the opinion of reporters. In the second game, another hard-fought 1-1 draw against Blackburn Rovers, it was easy to see how good defending 'kept Rovers in it. Bamford was the more polished back, with Fox unyielding, and both made timely last ditch interventions'. John Coe observed that, 'Bamford was full of resource and looked after left-winger Glover like a brother'. Rovers nearly snatched victory at the end, the Blackburn right back unconventionally stopping a goal by Vic Lambden by sitting on the ball.

In contrast, Rovers' first home game in the new division in front of a record evening crowd for an evening game of 28,173, dubbed the 'Battle of the Rovers' as the visitors were Doncaster, was something of a damp squib. Five hours of torrential rain fell beforehand and the 5,000 people waiting for the turnstiles to open were let in early so they could find some shelter. Disappointingly, Bristol Rovers, who had won 17 corners to Doncaster's three in the first half, lost 1-0 to a rare defensive lapse in the 66th minute. The Eastville crowd was finally able to cheer themselves hoarse when the 'No Buy Team met the Big Spenders' of Derby County on 29 August and triumphed 3-0, opening with an audacious chipped goal from Barrie Meyer, in a game where Rovers could have scored six and the referee was laid out when he took the full force of a clearance on his head. Frustratingly, it was followed by another narrow defeat to Doncaster. The *Pink 'Un*'s judgement was that while the defence and the half-back line was playing well, the forward line was not knitting together.

The same paper carried a comment piece by Pat Kavanagh: 'The Rovers are Learning Fast to Play Against the "Second Division Way"', which was a revealing look at the difference in modes of play between the Third and the Second Divisions and the role that the Rovers' men had in adjusting to them. 'Any morning you like to go out to Eastville these days,' commented Kavanagh, 'you will find Bristol Rovers' Debating Society in full swing. The young men who have made such a name for themselves in the sporting world in recent years have gone back to school – they are giving themselves a further education course in football'. After three matches, the Rovers team had sorted out largely for themselves how they should be adapting their tactics to the new style of play. Better teams in the Third Division used what the article referred to as 'the spearhead type of attack – long, raking passes producing fast raids by a couple of forwards, with perhaps a wing half closely backing up'. This was the style that had won Rovers promotion. However, most teams in the Second Division used the 'group attack system'. This involved all five forwards coming through together, perhaps backed up by both wing halves. If the centre-forward found himself too far forward of his inside men, he would come back to join the group. The challenge for Rovers was to find ways of combating the group attack and to use it themselves. Bert Tann claimed that he was having very little input into this process: 'I hardly needed to tell them anything. I have never heard any group of footballers talk more among themselves about tactics than these did after the Fulham match.'

The games which followed showed that adjustment was slowly taking hold. A very pleasing 3-0 away victory over old Third Division South adversaries Brentford, Geoff Bradford stealing the limelight from player-manager Tommy Lawton's side with a hat-trick, was followed by a 2-0 win over Bury and a storming fightback from two goals down against West Ham at Eastville on 12 September. By the end of the match, Noel Cantwell, one of four West Ham players on the pitch who were later to become managers of top flight clubs (Cantwell [Coventry City and others]; Dave Sexton and Frank O Farrell [Manchester United] and Malcolm Allison [Manchester City and Rovers] the other three) was reduced to kicking the ball over the stand into the River Frome to waste time. It cost Rovers one shilling for a boat to retrieve a ball lost like this, something which the papers remarked had not happened in a long while.

Bert Tann discusses tactics with Harry, Geoff Bradford and Jackie Pitt in the Rovers' dressing room

Two unexpected defeats by two of the weaker teams in the division followed. Bury, without a win before then, managed to score three against a Rovers' side for which nothing went right, Ray Warren ballooning a penalty over the bar and Harry heading out an inswinging cross which had gone over the head of Radford, only for the referee to award a goal. Rovers also lost by a single goal to Lincoln City after dominating the game, the usually reliable Warren missing another penalty. In both matches no blame was apportioned to the defence by the Bristol local press, which pointed instead to the problems of the attack. For the next game against Notts County away on 26 September, Geoff Bradford was to lead the attack instead of Vic Lambden. Rovers had not appeared at Meadow Lane since 1949, but six of their current players had turned out then, Harry included. It was a triumphant return, Bradford bagging a hat-trick among Rovers' five goals – and it could have been more as a goal was disallowed and Warren again missed from the spot. The ageless Warren in his 18th season was by common consent to be Rovers' player of the season, but Bert Tann regretfully decided that as Warren had missed four out of his last six penalties Bradford would take over that responsibility. October opened with another win against Hull City, 4-2, the Hull goalkeeper jumping high to pull down a shot from Harry at the end.

Despite most of the Eastville defence's members being at or nearing what Pat Kavanagh in the *Pink 'Un* described as 'the veteran stage in age', it seems to have quickly made a name for itself, despite the fears of many Rovers' fans that it would not stand the pace against faster, more precise forwards. Kavanagh reported that there was a general feeling that 'there is no rear section better than this in Division II and few, if any, better in the first', particularly because of their 'lightning speed in covering and recovery, the way they have found time and space to turn defence into attack… Harry Bamford and Geoff Fox, neither of them youngsters, have done everything any club could ask of them'.

The Hull game was the only Rovers' win in October, where they drew three and lost once; the first of the draws against Leeds at Elland Road came after they had taken a 3-1 lead before the break. Harry started the second half with plaster covering his right eye and was involved in some desperate defending as Leeds pressed for the winner. Then Harry and Jackie Pitt played Birmingham City's £65,000 forward line out of the game, but Rovers' forwards were denied time after time by Gil Merrick, Birmingham's England international keeper and the final score was 1-1. At this stage the plaudits given to the defence were still borne out by the statistics. If the seven goals conceded in the two early games against Fulham and Bury were ignored, Rovers had only let in 13 goals in 12 games. However, injuries were to play their part in putting a dent in their relative success. Against second in the table Nottingham Forest on 24 October, Geoff Fox was injured after 15 minutes and was a passenger for the rest of the game. Bryan Bush put Rovers in the lead with a 38 minute penalty, but Fox's problem meant that Rovers had to adopt a dour defensive strategy, playing long passes up to Geoff Bradford for relief. Eventually the stalwart resistance of Warren, Pitt and Bamford, who 'were all on top form' was broken and Forest scored three goals in the second half.

After 120 consecutive first team appearances, Harry's full-back partner Fox missed a 3-3 draw against Luton, where Rovers were again effectively reduced to 10 men after Bush was injured in the 20th minute. Barry Watkins again deputised for Fox in a second consecutive 3-3 draw against Plymouth Argyle on 7 November, described as 'the roughest, toughest game they have had so far in Division Two', where Rovers' season received a serious blow. Five minutes after the restart, Geoff Bradford was badly hurt in a tackle and was taken to hospital with a serious injury to his right knee, a chipped bone and other internal damage.

Harry rose magnificently to the occasion and was 'on great form', saving a certain goal when he headed a goal-bound Plymouth shot over the bar. Argyle protested vehemently that he had actually punched the ball out, but the referee consulted the linesman and waved away their protests. Rovers were not just hanging on: Bush had the ball in the net twice in the last ten minutes only to have both 'goals' disallowed.

November only saw the Rovers' injury crisis deepen and the *Evening Post* on the 28th of that month reported that it was their heaviest casualty list since the war. Against Rotherham on the 21st, when John McIlvenny twisted his knee after 10 minutes so badly that he limped through the rest of the game, Rovers had been effectively reduced to 10 men for most or part of the five games out of the last six. This bad luck forced Rovers into once again adopting a 'drab and dull' defensive style of play. With 15 minutes left to go, Harry and Geoff Fox shone in a grim battle, Harry making two fine interceptions to cut out scoring chances in the 'dark, closing minutes'. Few goals were conceded that month, but few were scored and there was, yet again, only one win.

Despite a 'lucky' win over Fulham, where Charlie Mitten again got the better of Harry, Rovers lost three out of four in December, to mutterings from unhappy fans about the standard of football. A 2-1 defeat at Eastville on the 19th by Blackburn Rovers (whom Bristol Rovers had also drawn in the Cup), the Lancashire side fielding five internationals, was described in the *Evening World* as 'one of the dullest

Sharp dressed men: Rovers' on a training walk: L-R Harry Bamford, Paddy Hale, Geoff Fox, Ray Warren, Josser Watling, Jack Pitt, Chick Cairney, George Petherbridge, Barrie Meyer, Bill Roost, Howard Radford and Peter Sampson

matches seen at Eastville this season'. The forwards were 'letting the side down… We had, too, the peculiar instance of Bamford taking the ball through and squaring for Fox to take the shot, with the forwards looking helpless.' Blackburn's winner came when their left-winger, ex-England international and Harry's team mate in Australia, Bobby Langton 'for a change, got around Bamford' to slip a ball to future Blackburn manager Eddie Quigley who shot low past Radford. A 4-0 Christmas day drubbing by promotion-chasing Everton, the heaviest defeat for Rovers since they lost by the same margin to Norwich in 1949 was followed three days later by a creditable 0-0 draw with Everton in front of a packed Eastville, the 34,015 crowd, the second best in Rovers' history, watching the 'Old Firm' in defence securing a point with an outstanding resistance.

Rovers took their one-win-a-month form into the New Year, beating Derby County away with a solitary goal from Paddy Hale, despite a heavily concussed Geoff Fox having to be led off the pitch at half-time by Ray Warren. Fox said afterwards that he could remember nothing of the last hour of the game. Both Rovers and City were at home for their Cup-ties next Saturday, a combined total of 43,335 attending, but Rovers lost 1-0 against Blackburn on 9 January, conceding in the 15th minute and failing to convert many scoring chances, having only scored two goals in their last five games. With their sharpshooters Bradford, Lambden and Bush all injured, Rovers depended on the defence again to keep Blackburn out on a 'glue pot' of a pitch. According to the *Evening Post*, 'Harry Bamford, the best back on the field, again had the measure of the international winger Bobby Langton. The pair had many hard but sporting tussles.' The *Evening World* thought that 'Harry Bamford had one of his best games ever, particularly after the interval, but all the good work was wasted out front'. The following League game was a 0-0 home stalemate against Brentford. Indeed, in the final 11 League games of the season Rovers only scored more than one goal in two matches, both wins, only losing twice but drawing three games 1-1. Not even a week's special training at Bournemouth could improve matters.

A frustrating January ended with a friendly against the 'Babes' of Manchester United, who had been knocked out of the Cup by Burnley, a game which the Rovers, according to the Bristol papers, were unlucky to lose. Bert Tann played his own Babes, 17 year olds Norman Sykes and Alfie Biggs and 23-year-old Ian Muir. Harry was facing another 32-year-old, Jack 'The Gunner' Rowley, who got his nickname from his quick-fire shooting which made him one of only four United players to score over 200 goals for the club. 'Traveller' in the *Post* wrote proudly: 'Rowley, one of United's internationals, is still a useful forward, but on Saturday he was generally held by Harry Bamford. I rated Bamford as the best of the full-backs. His positional play, quick tackling and clever interceptions were outstanding features of a really fine display.' Bob Bennett's cartoon made reference to the 'polar' conditions at Eastville (it snowed during the game and taps and rivers were frozen solid all over the city), suggesting that Rovers followed the lead of 'nearby winter sports enthusiasts... Harry Bamford would have been a match for one [a sleigh], even complete with reindeer. He was so at home in the snow that he stands a good chance of being picked for the next Everest expedition and, no doubt, will take along Muir, Sykes and Biggs – as Sherpas!'

Harry's prowess on ice was again on show next Saturday when Alfie Biggs made his league debut proper against Lincoln City away in 'skating rink conditions'. Harry's positioning meant that he made several

BRISTOL ROVERS FOOTBALL CLUB,
LIMITED

BRISTOL ROVERS

v.

MANCHESTER UNITED

SATURDAY, JANUARY 30th, 1954
Kick-off 2.45 p.m.

Official Souvenir Programme - 3d.

The programme for the friendly against Manchester United which Rovers' lost 1-0

timely interventions of shots which otherwise may have found the back of the net. In the first half when his keeper Radford had rushed out to intercept a corner and missed the ball, Harry, standing on the line cool as a cucumber, flicked the oncoming ball into Radford's hands as he scrambled back. With five minutes to go, with Radford once again stranded, he kicked out of harm's way what looked like a certain equaliser for the Imps. One noticeable feature of the match reports was Harry's cool clearances, often on the goal line – in the home draw against Notts County on 13 February Pat Kavanagh even said that 'Bamford was a little too cool sometimes for my liking', but that he kept the County left flank well under control 'and was as constructive as we expect the impeccable Harry to be'. As the Rovers' wing-halves were not very effective in this game – Sampson was not at his best and Pitt sustained an early injury – the link between defence and attack had to be provided by both full-backs, who worked hard to provide the service to the forwards only for it to be frittered away.

As frustration among the supporters about the lack of goals and what some felt was a 'negative and unattractive' style of football mounted, the old chestnut about Harry's best position was revived by a letter to the *Evening World*, calling for him to be moved to centre-forward. However, when Rovers did finally manage their first home win in four months against fourth in the table Nottingham Forest on 13 March, John Coe in the *Post* pointed out the advantages of a solid defence. From 16 away games Rovers had taken 15 points, only one fewer than League leaders Leicester City and were only one of two teams in the division to have conceded fewer goals than Leicester. Bert Tann did concede, though, that the disenchanted supporters had a point. Pat Kavanagh put it to him in a full-page interview that Rovers' style had changed. Before they 'positively banged the ball with such accuracy at one another… now they are inclined to fiddle, the ball slides from one player to another, often without any headway being made, and opposing defences are given ample opportunity to step in and intercept'. But Tann, although he agreed that his players should speed up, didn't accept they should return to their old style. The inexperience of the younger players that he had brought in up front meant that the half-backs and full-backs, unsure whether the man in front would be in position, were not releasing the ball as quickly. It had taken mature forwards two years to assimilate the 'fast direct style which Mr Tann calls "Up and Down"'.

Meanwhile, Harry had become part of the Players' Committee which had been formed to report back on suggestions arising out of informal meetings of players – 'the football equivalent of a works' committee in a factory'. The other members were Ray Warren, Geoff Fox, Vic Lambden, Frank Allcock and Josser Watling. The suggestions ranged from light training on Fridays, which was previously a non-training day, to the purchase of floating soap for the communal baths to prevent so much being wasted as it sank to the bottom, an idea which saved £3 a week. There were plenty of new ideas circulating around Eastville. Tann, prompted by the 6-3 thrashing of England's national team by Hungary, was going to the World Cup in Switzerland with a cine camera to record training and match play from around the globe which he hoped could be used to improve English football. He had also employed Mr. Douglas Paling, Bachelor of Science and Mathematics, a schoolmaster at St. Luke's College, Exeter, to produce a statistical analysis of all Rovers' matches. Tann commented: 'With the present Continental competition, we can no longer be satisfied with the old assumption that a good player is born, not made'. Mr. Paling concluded that Rovers' trademark long accurate passes switching play from one end to another were most effective from defence to wing and that young players were inaccurate in their passing over 20 yards. Harry Bamford was found to be usually highly accurate over both short and long distances and Tann could use the results of the reports to help his young players learn from the best, for example to emulate Harry's accuracy.

The season ended with something of an anti-climax. Rovers, to the game's only goal, suffered their first defeat since Christmas Day on 3 April away against Leicester, soon to become Second Division Champions, who were given 'half-time gas', oxygen, yet another new fad, despite Harry cutting off 'pass after pass… and giving a fine service to the forwards'. Harry, up to then ever-present, once again missed out on the last two games of the season and the Gloucestershire Cup after pulling a groin muscle against Swansea Town on 17 April. Still, the final game, a 3-2 home victory against Swansea, was marked by the welcome return of Geoff Bradford, who ended the Rovers' first season in the Second Division on a high note with a hat-trick. The *Evening World* in their season's review concluded that the team had, in the absence of Bradford for so long, done well to finish 9th in the table. 'The Rovers' defence proved itself one of the best in the whole Football League. They blotted forward line after forward line, brilliant though some of them were on paper, into comparative ineffectiveness.'

Harry recovered in time for the ten day post-season tour of Eire in May, playing in two of the games, including the 3-2 victory over an All Star Irish XI in front of 30,000, which was then the biggest ever soccer crowd in Dublin. He had, however, one more match of his own before the summer began.

Harry's Greatest Match

Harry Bamford was passing the time on Victoria Street which runs today from the Temple Circus gyratory to Bristol Bridge, buying the evening paper and stopping for a while to chat to the seller. Victoria Street was the obvious route back to the Marsh for someone who worked in the centre of Bristol, and Harry spotted someone he knew well, who grew up in St. Silas Street, just round the corner from his family home in Moor Street and who worked as a shorthand typist for Distillers in the city, Violet Boon. Harry offered to walk Violet home and on the way he asked her if she would like to go out with him. Violet said no, but some months later, she changed her mind.

Of course, Harry could have met Violet purely by chance that December day in 1952. However, he was never the most impulsive of people and it is more than possible that, knowing she made this journey regularly, he was deliberately waiting for her, taking the opportunity of speaking to her away from neighbours' scrutiny. Violet was a pretty, petite brunette with striking, luminous blue eyes, the young widow of Harry Boon, once a well-known sporting figure in St. Philips who ran the St. Silas Boys Club, and the brother of Harry Bamford's long-time friend PC William Boon. Violet had wed Harry Boon in 1947 when she was 22, but their marriage was cut short by her husband's tragic early death four years later in 1951 from blood poisoning following a football injury. Violet told her daughter Hilary that while he was lying in bed during his illness, Harry Boon had steered her gently in the direction of his friend the other Harry, saying pointedly more than once: 'That Harry Bamford, now he's a nice chap'.

Although she had been married to a talented amateur footballer and members of her family, the Holveys (dad Bert ran a fruit and vegetable

The wedding party on the steps of St. Mary Redcliffe. To the left of Harry are his mother Daisy and father Harry. Behind Harry is the vicar and behind him is his brother Ron. Behind Ron is youngest brother Alan. Next to Violet are her father Bert Holvey and her mother Violet.

shop on the corner of St. Silas Street in the Marsh), used to watch Rovers regularly, Violet knew nothing about the game, something which only added to her attractiveness for Harry. She said later that: 'Harry used to say that if I had been a football supporter he wouldn't have asked me out'.

Six months or so after their meeting on Victoria Street, Violet and Harry started seeing each other and she accompanied him to the Bristol Rovers promotion dinner in May 1953. While his other team mates married around him, Harry had remained the bachelor of the squad, until, on Saturday 22 May 1954, at the age of 34, he stood on the steps of the south porch of the magnificent St. Mary Redcliffe Church arm in arm with Violet, who, as a widow, chose to wear a smart suit for the occasion. Lined up proudly alongside the happy couple in the wedding

The bride and groom

photographs are the members of the Bamford and Holvey families. Bristol Rovers were represented by captain Ray Warren, club chairman Herbert Hampden Alpass and Eric Godfrey the chair of the Supporters' Club.

The wedding made the front pages of some of the local papers. The *Evening World* under the headline 'Smile They Waited For' had a photograph of the happy couple being showered with confetti by Ray Warren as they left the church, Harry giving 'one of his rare smiles' and looking as if he could not believe his luck. The paper also described Violet as a childhood friend and revealed that the couple would be moving away from the Marsh to a new home in Richmond Road, Montpelier. This was a club flat on the first floor. Harry commented: 'My marriage will make no difference to my football plans. We plan to stay in Bristol. I shall probably play for the Rovers another three seasons before retiring from the game. I have no settled ideas about what I shall do then, but I may take up bricklaying or something in the building line as I have some training in that kind of work.'

As was mentioned in the previous chapter, Harry's plans for his future after football began to take a very different direction from the building trade. No doubt encouraged by Bert Tann, but also by his own preferences, he decided to study for his Preliminary Coaching Certificate. In the family papers his FA Coaching record book is preserved, a slim maroon volume with the Three Lions badge and 'The Football Association Coaching Certificate' picked out in gold on the cover. This reveals that he attended an FA course at Exeter in 1953, before taking his Preliminary Coaching Examination in Bristol in 1954. On 27 September 1954, he received a letter from FA Headquarters at Lancaster Gate giving him the good news that he had passed the following subjects, giving grades for each: Practical Coaching: Good; Practical Performance: Average; Theory of Coaching: Satisfactory; Laws of the Game: Good. Enclosed with it were his certificate and a lapel badge, both of which also survive. There is a photograph of Harry in the Class of '54 taken on the lawn at the National Recreation Centre at Lilleshall Hall in Shropshire with Walter Winterbottom and England

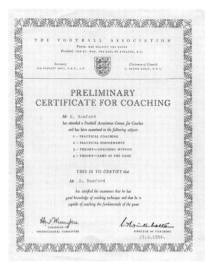

Harry's preliminary coaching certificate

Confirmation Harry had passed his full certificate in 1955

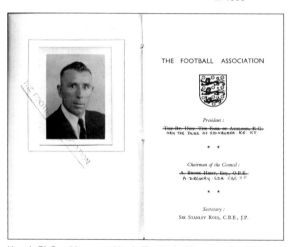

Harry's FA Coaching record book. The FA thriftily crossed out outdated information rather than reprinting

Harry's FA Coach official lapel badges

captain Billy Wright in the middle of the front row. The FA held its summer schools there after 1948. Harry took other courses, according to his pass book: a CCPR (Centre for the Council of Physical Recreation) course at Bristol in 1954 and another FA Course EC/55 at Exeter in 1955. A second letter in 1955 confirmed that he had qualified for his full coaching certificate. In the same year he was officially appointed to the Somerset and Gloucestershire coaching panels. Nowadays 'doing your badges' as professional footballers call studying for UEFA coaching licences, is commonplace, but in the 1950s those taking training courses were forward thinking pioneers, sometimes held up for ridicule by their peers who believed that footballing talent was innate and could not be taught.

Harry was obviously a diligent student. Some of his course notes survive, meticulously written in biro in his neat, backwards-sloping script, traditionally, according to handwriting experts, a sign of someone who likes to keep themselves to themselves. In the lectures he attended there was a clear emphasis on imparting the 'skills of the game', 'the basis from which we should start teaching schoolboys'. There are drills and exercises in various skills from heading to tackling, and sections on pressure training so that these skills can be applied in stressful situations. A modern former Premier League professional footballer who looked over some of these notes commented that the methods being employed would not be out of place in the present day game. F. H. Stanlake of Holsworthy AFC in Devon who attended several courses with Harry and became a friend described him later as 'a keen student of the game. He would apply his mind to books on soccer with the same endeavour that he showed on the field of play during the various coaching courses'.

Bert Tann was not only a keen advocate of his players studying coaching, he had come back from the World Cup in Switzerland in 1954 brimming with fresh ideas for his team. He had observed that the Hungarians and South Americans used many of the same techniques he had brought to Rovers, but also played all the year round, enabling them to assimilate what they were taught more thoroughly. Tann became convinced that the English game needed to curtail its lengthy close

The Class of '54. Walter Winterbottom, England manager and the FA's director of coaching and Billy Wright, England and Wolves captain, are to the left of the man in the all-white tracksuit in the front row. Harry is near the centre in the third row wearing a white shirt

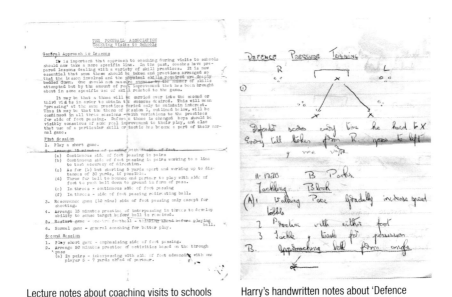

Lecture notes about coaching visits to schools

Harry's handwritten notes about 'Defence Pressure Training'

season. Hence the 'revolutionary "PT by the seaside" plan' which he unveiled in the local press on 23 July, designed to make Rovers one of the fittest sides in the country. The team would be spending a fortnight under canvas at Uphill Road sports ground in Weston-super-Mare from the beginning of August. Some 33 players would live and sleep in a huge marquee 40 feet x 20 feet laid out with camp beds. Those who had served in the Forces like Harry or were on National Service would be familiar with the potato peeling and 'normal chores of camp life' they were expected to share. But the main aim was to be able to put the team through two stiff sessions of physical training and ball practice every day in front of the public. As Tann put it: 'This is a serious plan to improve our concentration and our mental and physical standards. It is not a stunt. We want our players to think as footballers and athletes for twenty-four hours a day'. Rovers also invited youths between 13 and 19 to apply to take part in special coaching sessions in association with the Somerset FA Youth section which would be held on six evenings and could cater for between 100-150 boys. Harry particularly enjoyed coaching the local youngsters who turned up, commenting: 'I feel it does me good to pass on something to these boys'.

Wives, children and girlfriends had no place there, but the married men were allowed to go home to their families at the weekend. Being a footballer's wife, as Violet soon found out, was by no means glamorous and wives were kept firmly away from the business of football. If she went to watch Harry play, Violet, and the other wives, had to wait for their husbands by the players' entrance, Violet longer than the rest because Harry did not like to come out until things had quietened down.

Unfortunately, in the grand tradition of English Bank Holidays, a freak storm swept the West Country on 2 August, making the holiday 'one of the dreariest ever known'. The *Evening World* stationed reporter John Moger at the camp, who commented that many of the players, with foresight, had brought extra blankets. Harry was pictured on the front page of the paper on 3 August getting stuck into training rather than spending time with his new bride. In his Foreword, Josser Watling, who was then still recovering from a cartilage operation, remembers fondly the comradeship of this camp and the happy times spent singing around his mother's portable organ, but he is not so complimentary about the mountains of salad. Not everyone in the football world was convinced by the latest Tann Plan which was mocked in some quarters, big pundits apparently 'laughing their heads off'.

1954-55 was to be one of those 'difficult second seasons' for the Rovers, after they had been the new boys in the Second Division the previous term. The arrangement of the League fixture programme meant that nearly every club would have completed a quarter of their matches by the last week in September, with two matches a week placing a strain particularly on the smaller squads of the clubs in the lower divisions. After its temporary post-war boom, football in general was in the doldrums, perturbed by the 4,500,000 fall in attendances since 1946. Spurred on by an outbreak of slow hand-clapping at grounds all over the country (but not at Eastville) in the first few matches of the season, directors and managers of all 92 clubs issued an assurance that their teams, according to Pat Kavanagh, would place the emphasis on

Harry and Ray Warren coaching boys at Weston during the Rovers' summer training camp

'intelligently planned attacking football, rather than on the concentrated defence that had marred so much soccer since the late Herbert Chapman introduced the third-back system to Highbury'. As we have seen, Harry always saw himself, much to the consternation of some of his fans, as an attacking back and he would probably have had little to argue about over the pledge that full-backs would push forward. Whether Ray Warren would be transformed into an attacking pivot as proposed was less certain, but, as Mike Jay and Stephen Byrne in their definitive official history of Bristol Rovers have pointed out, this season the club's defensive record was its worst since 1948.

Rovers had no need to worry about declining attendances in their opening game against Port Vale on 21 August. The front pages of the local papers carried photographs of police preventing spectators from invading the pitch and sections of the bumper 32,367 Eastville gate were 'unruly' during the game, problems arising because of overcrowding in some sections and latecomers trying to gain access through jammed entrances. The match itself was unremarkable, the visitors keeping a tight rein on Rovers and launching few attacks themselves, before Bradford scored what sports reporters in those days used to call a 'picture goal' to give Rovers a deserved, but narrow 1-0 win.

Harry, like Rovers, took time to find his form this season. After the opening victory, Rovers found themselves conceding goals in their August games and having to stage heroic fightbacks to rescue a point. Things improved in September, which began with two convincing victories, only one goal conceded, and two Geoff Bradford hat-tricks, against an injury-hit Derby County and Liverpool, the latter relegated from the First Division the previous season. Geoff Fox was injured and his place at left-back was taken by Les Edwards. Edwards won praise but the rest of the defence, aside from Ray Warren, was under the microscope. Local reporter Gordon Shoreham commented: 'Any criticism of the Rovers' defence must be based on the high standard they set for themselves last year. On this assessment Bamford has yet to find his best form, Sampson, after a grand first half, could do little right in the second and Pitt, who seldom has a bad match, has still to recapture his former brilliance.' Against Liverpool, 'Bamford was way below his best,' but also there were signs that 'he is beginning to get over the bad patch which comes to all good players at some stage of their career, and formed a good understanding with a much improved Pitt'.

Unfortunately, in the next two games, both away against West Ham and Liverpool again, Rovers let in ten goals to lose both. As a thunderstorm raged on 11 September, Harry Hooper, West Ham's England prospect, ripped Edwards and the rest of the Rovers' left flank apart in a 'one man dazzle' which saw him bag one goal and make the other four. Both the *Liverpool Daily Post* and Bristol's *Evening World* were in agreement that Harry had made a herculean effort to rescue the next game at Anfield, with Ray Warren a passenger on the left wing with a bandaged right knee and rampant Liverpool forward 'Long' John Evans scoring four of their five goals to put his side 4-1 up just after half-time. After Peter Hooper made it 4-2, Leslie Edwards of the local Liverpool paper enthused: 'full-back Bamford, a giant of a man whose head had

LIVERPOOL - BRISTOL ROVERS

EVENING EXPRESS—Saturday, September 18, 1954   7

GOALMOUTH THRILLERS

Full-back Bamford beats Ashcroft for Bristol's third

After jinking his way past three defenders Harry scores a cracking goal against Liverpool on 11 September 1954

been damaged earlier in the game, came to inside-right and jinked his way cheekily through three defenders to make the score 4-3 at the 81st minute.' Pat Kavanagh was not to be outdone: 'Bamford, playing a great game, probed deeply and consistently into Liverpool territory. This was the old Harry, the immaculate distributor of the ball, occasionally taking a chance but making some wonderful openings. The full-back capped a fine performance by going through on his own to score the best goal of the match, a feat which astounded the 31,100 spectators.' John Coe in the *Evening Post* was disappointed that, after 'Bamford had shown the way', to loud applause from Liverpool and Rovers' fans alike, there was not an 'all-out assault' on the Liverpool goal, but that Rovers conceded the initiative to lose 5-3.

Manager Johnny Carey, a big Bamford admirer, emphasised Harry's contribution to the defeat of his Blackburn Rovers team on 18 September at Eastville. 'Our best forward this season has been Bobby Langton, He didn't get a chance because Harry Bamford… timed his tackles so well. Bamford's was a fine exhibition of defensive skill,' or as Pat Kavanagh put it, 'the brilliant Bobby was subdued by an equally brilliant Harry Bamford'. When Les Edwards was dropped at left-back and long-standing Rovers' part-timer Barry Watkins was drafted in to resume his partnership with Harry from the early days, along with Ian Muir as understudy for Warren at centre-half, there were fears that Rovers might struggle in their final game of the month against Fulham. Rovers drew the biggest gate – 31,648 – in the Second Division that day, one of Fulham's officials stating: 'Bristol Rovers are getting a reputation for providing thrills. Our supporters like them a lot.' Harry, of course, renewed his battle with Charlie Mitten at Craven Cottage and commentators reckoned that honours were even. Rovers' reorganised defence played their part in their 'shock' 3-2 victory, as did Rovers' attack, Barrie Meyer scoring a brace and Bradford getting the other after a three-game barren spell.

Bert Tann, on the back of two straight victories, felt able to counter some criticism about Rovers' defensive style. Pat Kavanagh called this 'fiddling… a pass from left-back to right-back, to right-half and then over to left-back with no ground gained or lost.' Tann argued this was a deliberate tactic used to keep possession of the ball until an accurate pass could be made to another player in a good position', in other words keeping possession and playing out from the back. 'Admittedly a long kick, although it may be chancy, is more heart-warming to the supporter who wants lots of action, but it hampers accuracy and I believe that in the long run the system of the defensive inter-passing is the best'. More vindication came when 'goal-hungry Rovers' equalled their biggest-ever post-war League victory, putting in seven goals against Swansea without reply at Eastville, where a large replica of a swan was placed in the centre of the pitch by an away supporter before kick off. Harry did not appear on the score sheet again, despite finding time to go up into the attack himself during the game.

The following 3-2 victory on 9 October against Luton at Eastville took Bristol Rovers, without captain Ray Warren who was in the Reserves for the first time since the war, to their highest position ever, second in the Second Division. The tables were turned when top of the League Rotherham United 'played like champions and the Rovers' defence was overrun.' Harry had a torrid afternoon from the start in the 6-2 drubbing, nutmegged by a shot in the third minute which almost led to a goal and the splendidly-named inside-forward Gladstone Guest lobbing the ball over his head twice. Subsequent results were inconsistent. Rovers were a free-scoring side, scoring 28 goals at home in nine games and by 6 November unbeaten at Eastville since 19 December 1953, but their away form was letting them down. On 6 November when an 'unsteady' Rovers defence conceded two first half goals against Lincoln, Harry and Jackie Pitt struggling to hold Lincoln's left flank, before a fight back saw the game end level, there were only three teams in the four English divisions which had scored more goals than Rovers. But they had taken only two points from their seven away games. Attention began to focus on the age of the Rovers' defence, but Pat Kavanagh opined that the problem was rather that the forwards, while they had flourished in attack, were not providing enough cover for the defence which was finding itself overwhelmed when an attack broke down.

Bert Tann professed himself unperturbed, pointing out the Rovers were still only four points behind Rotherham. His solution was to bring in Mr. Al Murray, the official coach of the Great Britain and Switzerland weight-lifting teams, to add variety in training. Murray devised a six-week training programme with light weights to enable the team to kick the ball harder and faster. A good away win against Hull City was prompted by Jackie Pitt and Harry, 'the perfect Pitt-Bamford co-ordination, with the right-back pushing through these long inch-accurate passes' throughout the game, Frank Allcock now partnering Harry at left-back. Rovers went back up to third place in the table on 20 November with a 4-0 win against Ipswich, before losing by a single goal to Nottingham Forest, the first time they had failed to score this season, despite Harry playing in Geoff Bradford several times with well-paced passes. Fortunately, the game was away at the City ground, because the Frome had flooded once more, water swirling into the club buildings and onto the terraces, although a concerted effort with buckets and

3,000 sandbags largely kept the pitch safe.

Promotion began to be talked about seriously, but Rovers lapsed into another December slump, failing to win a single game, drawing once and scoring only two goals in their five games. Rovers finally lost a home game, after remaining unbeaten at Eastville for a year, on 27 December, the second of consecutive defeats by Notts County sending them tumbling into the lower half of the division to 12th place. Harry was at fault for the goal which started the 4-1 rout, losing the ball from a Petherbridge throw in to a County forward who promptly ran clear of the Rovers' defence to roll the ball past Howard Radford. New Year's Day brought respite with Rovers' first victory in seven weeks and what turned out to be the temporary return of Fox at left-back, although Harry once again had supporters on the edge of their seats when just before half-time he very nearly lost the ball when only a couple of yards from his own goal.

One explanation for the decline in Rovers' form was that Tann's 'Continental Plan' of keeping possession was not working on Britain's sticky winter pitches. Certainly Rovers had played on some mud baths such as the pitch at Port Vale on 18 December which was judged to have outdone even 'the old Eastville pitch at its worst', with deep grey mud and pools of water, topped by several inches of sand. Harry joked as the team walked past it to the dressing room to change for the match, 'We want Big Brother if we are going to do anything on that,' probably referring to some kind of tractor rather than *1984*. The defence had tightened up, as one supporter writing to the *Pink 'Un* observed. 'Harry Bamford is still the best ball player in the side but his speed is not what it was, and Harry must remember that if he goes up too far with the ball he will take longer to get back. It will be a sad loss to Eastville when Harry hangs up his boots.' There is a hand-written message to Harry on this clipping in the family archives in pencilled capital letters: 'GOOD LUCK GO WITH YOU – MUM & DAD'. Another letter to the paper was less diplomatic. 'The senior members in defence must realise that their slowing down in pace entails a greater use of the longer ball. Their experience makes these particular players still valued members of the side, but their loss of speed can only be remedied by cutting out the elaborate footwork in their own area and by less roaming into their opponents' territory.'

Attention turned away from the League with the return of the FA Cup on 8 January 1955, an eagerly-awaited tie against First Division Portsmouth. In front of 35,921 and after a few days at Weston training in deep snow, the 'Old Faithfuls', nine of the eleven who had drawn 0-0 against Newcastle four years previously, including long-term absentee Vic Lambden, 'took the pomp out of Pompey'. A goal down after 62 minutes, Rovers quickly hit back, Bradford equalising two minutes later and Roost grabbing the winner five minutes after that. Harry and the rest of the team were pictured on the *Evening World*'s front page, gathered round the radio in their training jerseys and shorts for the Cup draw to hear that Chelsea would be coming to Eastville in two weeks' time. 10,000 queued at the ground in snow nearly a foot deep on Saturday 15 January to attend the reserve game against QPR where a voucher enabling them to apply for a Cup ticket would be issued. Instead, like Rovers' away game against Derby County that day, the match was cancelled because of the previous day's blizzard, but John Gummow made the decision to issue the vouchers anyway. Four thousand at the back of the queue refused to leave empty-handed when all the 6,000 vouchers printed had been snapped up.

Cup fever seemed to have distracted everyone; the intervening match before the big day saw Rovers take 'a thrashing and a lesson in good football' 4-2 from West Ham, the 'old guard' in defence out-manoeuvred. Thousands trekked to Eastville to see Chelsea's first visit in 48 years, the two sides last meeting in a Western League match in the 1906-07 season, some getting up at 6am, although 50-year-old George Webber, who had bought a blue and white suit for the match, injured his chest at work and couldn't go. When the turnstiles opened, people rushed across the terraces 'like a huge army' in a race to secure the best viewpoint. The gulf in class soon became apparent, the Chelsea forwards 'tearing large holes in the slow-moving Rovers' defence' according to Joe Hulme writing in the *Sunday People*. As Chelsea went one-up after five minutes and added another two goals before half-time, the Rovers' defence often found themselves 'completely mesmerized'. After the restart the defence got to grips with the Chelsea forwards, but too late to affect the outcome, although Rovers never gave up and Pitt reduced the deficit in the 60th minute with a penalty. The following Wednesday, the Rovers' players went to the Gaumont Cinema to see the newsreel of their defeat. Ray Warren didn't find it comfortable viewing and commented as he left: 'They were three bad goals from our point of view and the defence was in a tangle on each occasion'. However, there were extenuating circumstances, Chelsea were on their way to becoming First Division Champions.

'Cup Glamour is All Very Nice – But Mr Tann's Eyes Are on League Problems' is how one newspaper headline brought things back down to earth. It was perhaps an exaggeration to suggest the team was facing relegation worries, as they were 12 points above bottom team Ipswich, but they had a very tough programme in the next six weeks, playing four of the five teams at the top of the table. Such was the open nature of the Second Division that Rovers were actually only nine points below leaders Luton Town. Two mainstays of the team were dropped for the next game – Geoff Bradford (at his own request) and Harry. Supporters dug out their pens when hearing the news, one of them, C. J. Downing from Yate reviving the old debate about Harry's best position. 'I have also read of the proposals to drop Bamford, the finest ball player in the team, though admittedly slower than he used to be. I suggest his inclusion at inside-right would bring further control to an attack sadly lacking in this respect, and his wonderful understanding with Pitt could be applied to attack as well as it has been in the past to the defence. This is indeed no time for the Rovers to resort to the popular game of Hunt the Scapegoat.'

Rovers then sustained their biggest defeat since before the war when Joe Payne had scored ten for Luton Town, losing away to Blackburn 8-3. Although Rovers were 3-2 up at half-time, after the break, their defence, with Fox taking Harry's place, crumbled. When the seventh Blackburn goal went in (the eighth was a penalty), the *Pink 'Un* observed: 'The

Rovers' defence had never looked so wide open'. For the following game against Fulham, Bert Tann was quick to restore Bradford and Harry who was prominent as the Rovers' defence put on a dour, tight display. Pat Kavanagh commented: 'I have never seen Bamford tackle so hard, or so accurately, as he did here. Mitten, a highly dangerous winger who on one of the few occasions he did get away made the goal for Johnny Haynes, was almost entirely blotted from the game.' Rovers won 4-1.

On 5 March, Rovers' defence helped secure a narrow yet valuable 1-0 win against Rotherham who had put six past them earlier in the season. The speedy and clever Rotherham wingers Jack Grainger and Ian Wilson looked like overwhelming the home side again, being fed by a series of long passes from their wing-halves, until Harry and Frank Allcock got wise to what was happening, tightening their grip on both wingers in the second half until they became ineffective. Peter Hooper's winner came late, eight minutes from time, but even then Rovers' defence, Harry included, made three vital clearances off the line before the final whistle.

Harry had already scored his goal for the season against Liverpool in September, but he was to double his tally in the strangest of circumstances on 26 March against Lincoln City at Sincil Bank. The *Pink 'Un* described it as a 'shock goal', observing: 'The Lincoln fans… will talk for a long time about that second Bristol Rovers' goal from the half-way line – it flabbergasted everyone, including goalkeeper [Mitchell] Downie and Bamford who scored it'. In the lead thanks to a Geoff Bradford goal, two minutes from time Harry, from the half-way line, lobbed a centre into the open space behind the Lincoln defence. The Lincoln goalkeeper Downie, his attention distracted by the close proximity of Bradford, completely misjudged the flight of the ball, dived too late and could only lay helpless as the ball slid by his fingers into the mud.'

Rovers' February recovery continued into March and April, but although they fought their way back to within three points of the leaders at one point, too much damage had been done to their League campaign by their mid-season slump. Harry continued his good form to the end of the season. Against Plymouth Argyle on 8 April he put on a show at Eastville, the crowd enjoying some of the warmest Easter temperatures for 17 years and Bamford 'right on the top of his game', making three passes in the first few minutes of 'international class'. Bert Tann rested him on 16 April, to make space for Geoff Fox, still trying to make a comeback, with Frank Allcock shifted to right-back.

Unfortunately, Rovers lost their chance of getting a share of the merit money paid to the top four finishers in the division thanks to a defeat at Stoke where the referee allowed the home side to dish out the rough stuff, leaving four Rovers players nursing injuries at the end. But the other Bristol team was basking in the glory. While Rovers, in front of their smallest gate for two years, 14,707, were held to a 2-2 draw at Eastville by Middlesbrough in the last league game of the season to finish 8th, having led 2-0 in the first half, champions Bristol City had equalled Nottingham Forest's Third Division record of 70 points in a season and scored their 100th goal on their way to join Rovers next season. Jackie Pitt and Harry were the only two Rovers players absolved from accusations of slackness in the final few matches. With 44 and 42 games respectively, and two goals apiece, the two close friends and on-pitch partners topped the appearance charts for the club.

City's promotion ensured the highest ever crowd, 20,097, for a hotly contested Gloucestershire Senior Cup Final on 2 May 1955, Harry doing his bit to make sure he took home a third winner's medal. Neither side wanted to lose, both defences kicking for touch or a corner at the slightest hint of danger, but eight minutes from time with Rovers leading 2-1, Howard Radford lost possession of a centre which was then shot towards his gaping goal. Harry made a last-ditch interception, hooking the ball away. Despite vehement claims from City players that the ball had crossed the line, Harry maintained his poker face and the referee waved the protestors away. The season ended with a flight to Jersey for a match against Portsmouth to commemorate the tenth anniversary of the ending of the German Occupation, the first ever game in the Channel Islands between Football League clubs. 'Bamford's many duels with [Gordon] Dale', the report read, 'were the highlight of a most

Proud parents; Harry
and Violet with baby
daughter Hilary

Hilary, now a toddler, sits on her mother's knee with doting dad Harry in close attendance, watched
by Violet's sister Eunice who was later to play a big part in Hilary's upbringing

Hilary and Harry in St. Andrew's Park

interesting match', which Rovers won, giving them a second victory over Pompey that season.

Harry had more than just the new season to look forward to as he and Violet were expecting a child. Their first daughter Hilary, weighing 7lb 8ozs was born on 13 October 1955, obligingly not on a match day, at Mount Hope Nursing Home on Ashley Hill, not far from the couple's flat in Montpelier. Mount Hope was run by the Salvation Army and took in unmarried pregnant women, but also accepted private patients, charging £10 for delivering a baby, money which it used to fund its charitable work. Harry was immediately smitten by the new arrival. It was unusual for a man to be seen pushing a pram in those days, but Harry took Hilary out every afternoon when he arrived back from training and a favourite spot was St. Andrew's Park. A family photograph shows Hilary sitting on the grass there with her doting Dad watching carefully over her.

CHAPTER 11

400 and More

Bert Tann gave an interview to the *Evening World* before the new 1955-56 season began in which he explained that he was preparing for the future in defence and was looking for men 'with the Harry Bamford touch', 'constructive full-backs who were not interested in the big kick downfield'. 'Who is to take the place of Bamford,' the paper asked, 'whose immaculate distribution plays such a big part in the team's tactics, when he finally retires or should he be unfortunate enough to be hurt?' The Scot Ian Muir, who had previously played at centre-half as a deputy for Ray Warren until Paddy Hale had been given the berth, was one possible successor touted. Geoff Fox had not been re-signed in the summer so Frank Allcock would continue to partner Harry at left back. The established and successful Rovers' defence was undergoing big changes through necessity. But Harry had clearly no intention of retiring any time soon. Indeed, when the Rovers' men reported back for training on 22 July, they found that three of their team mates, Harry, Jackie Pitt and Howard Radford were already in harness. Pitt had turned up two weeks early; Radford had been in two weeks light training after a cartilage operation. Harry, though, had been training at Eastville for the past six weeks, in line with Tann's thinking that too long a close season hampered English players' effectiveness. Not that he was neglecting his preparations for his post-football future, attending another FA coaching course at St Luke's College at Exeter at the end of July.

The Rovers' squad travelled to Weston for another two weeks under canvas, this time to sweat in temperatures of 70 plus degrees in the baking hot sun, put through their paces by trainer Fred Ford. A former team mate of Tann's at Charlton, Ford had been brought in because the increase in desk work Division Two entailed meant Tann couldn't devote as much time to training. Ford had introduced 100-minute practice matches so that playing for 90 would seem easier. There was some light relief. Harry was pictured in the local papers cooling off with some team mates in Weston's open-air swimming pool and Rovers provided a team for a six-a-side 'brighter cricket' tournament at Weston cricket ground which was televised. Rovers lost in the preliminary round (Harry was not part of the team), but the experience was so enjoyable that the players organised their own competition. There was some disappointment that no local youth clubs had responded to letters offering free football coaching.

The benefits of Harry's continuous summer training were obvious from the start. He and Jackie Pitt were praised time and time again for their 'astute anticipation' and 'skilful constructive passing' in the first nine games which saw only one defeat, with twenty goals scored, and put Rovers on top of the Second Division table for the first time ever on 29 August when they won 2-1 at Stoke City. Rovers had adopted a very exciting style of play with fast positional interchanges which opponents found difficult to cope with. A letter to the local paper from an impressed Stoke fan declared: 'Your boys are 100 per cent fit and full 90-minute men… Division I cannot be far away,' a belief which many Bristol Rovers' supporters began to share as the team hung on to the top spot.

Despite being responsible for a 'tragic mistake' in the Stoke game, which gifted the home side their goal, the *Evening Post*'s John Coe declared 'it is impossible to withhold praise from Bamford'. In the 60th minute, Harry had mystifyingly headed the ball straight to the feet of Stoke's inside-forward Eric Lowell who slammed the ball into the net, later explaining ruefully that he thought Lowell was Allcock, a vivid demonstration of the effect of having to adjust to a new full-back partner. Sheffield Wednesday on 3 September inflicted Rovers' first defeat of the season, but Wednesday, newly relegated from the First Division, had spent big to rebuild in the summer, signing striker Jackie Sewell who had toured with Harry in Australia, as well as Matt Busby's son-in-law Don Gibson. But it was 'quicksilver' striker and golden boy Albert Quixall who did the damage.

Rovers were back on track when they went to Anfield to take on Liverpool four days later, Leslie Edwards from the *Liverpool Post* once again dipping his pen in purple ink to report that 'these Bristol Rovers roved like masters and passed with the smoothness and accuracy of, say, a Spurs or Manchester United at their best… One could wish that either of our two senior teams could show such precise, close-linked movement as Bristol – not only in attack; but in combined operation in which goal-keeper, backs, half-backs and forwards were not so many separate departments but the team compleat… I have rarely seen a First Division side move so sweetly and with such certainty.' Singled out was 'that massive but conspicuously dainty back Bamford'. Harry's 'precision clearances under difficulties' drew roars of applause from the Liverpool crowd. Edwards also commented approvingly on Rovers' 'continental' practice of triangular passing between goalkeeper and backs. Towards the end of the game Howard Radford's boot split across the sole, but as captain Jackie Pitt couldn't afford him leaving the pitch to change it, Harry and Frank Allcock had to take the goal kicks instead. Some supporters who rang the *Evening World* office to find out the result didn't believe it when they were told Rovers had won 2-0.

More convincing victories followed and there was further recognition for the team with the news that the first full England cap for a Rovers' player would be awarded to Geoff Bradford in October. By the time Harry reached the milestone of his 400th game for Rovers, a 2-1 away victory against Hull City on 17 September, Rovers led the Division with a game in hand over nearest challengers Fulham and Stoke. The *Pink 'Un* marked Harry's achievement with a special article which claimed that a few weeks before one of England's selectors (with a lack of preparation which beggars belief) had approached Bert Tann after a match and asked some questions about their excellent right-back as he might be considered for an under-23 side. Tann tactfully said that he was afraid that the player in question was not eligible. 'No manager will ever get him to change his style,' the paper went on, 'He plays the game exactly as he sees it – and that means that every ball must be used to

Geoff Bradford shares a laugh with his good friend Harry

maximum effect. The fact is that Harry approaches his game with the viewpoint of the pure artist. There are few players in the country who reflect such credit on the game as he does.'

When Blackburn Rovers' visited Eastville's the following week, the 29,489 gate was only bettered in the Second Division by Liverpool. Harry had his usual good game against Bobby Langton, coming away with the ball cleanly in tackle after tackle, before deploying it accurately to Rovers' advantage. Bill Eckersley, the England left-back who has also been on tour with Harry in Australia, opined after the home 1-0 victory: 'I think that if the selectors had seen on him on this form he would get a cap'. Just when Rovers had put daylight between themselves and other teams at the top, they suffered three defeats in a row to drop them right down the table to fifth and put Bristol City above them. Two of these were consecutive away games; the vagaries of the fixture arrangements had given Rovers seven away games out of their first eleven matches. The first Bristol derby of the season was greeted with feverish excitement and a Bristol record League game attendance of 37,797, but it was a disappointing encounter, which ended honours even. Played at a breakneck speed, the quality suffered accordingly. City were now in second, Rovers still in fifth, but separated by a single point.

From the end of October, Rovers went on a goal spree. Four goals went in against Leeds, Barrie Meyer, Geoff Bradford (2) and Dai Ward finding their shooting boots. One commentator, Harry Ditton, pointed out that the glut of goals was partly thanks to the notable creative contribution made by the defence in which 'no one took the eye more than right-back Harry Bamford. The use he made of the ball would have done credit to a Johnny Haynes'. Fulham were on the receiving end next on Bonfire Night in an eight-goal match full of fireworks which was headed for a three-all draw until the 86th minute. Harry, refusing to be satisfied with a point, took the ball off his old adversary Charlie Mitten's toes 'as cool as a cucumber', raced forward and sent over a perfectly placed, high ball into the middle for Barrie Meyer to head home to give Rovers the lead for the third time and complete his hat-trick, before Geoff Bradford made it 5-3 a minute from time. The visiting Moscow Dynamo team was in the crowd and their representative commented that Bristol Rovers were 'a team without weaknesses'.

Against Bury the following Saturday, Rovers coasted to an easy 4-2 win. Harry, who had an 'unfortunate game', made a major contribution to the score line – at the wrong end – making one and scoring the other of Bury's two goals. On the 61st minute, he stuck out a foot but failed to clear the ball properly. Instead, it agonisingly rolled a yard behind him, presenting Bury's inside-forward Douglas Fletcher with the easiest of chances. Four minutes from the end, he deflected a harmless pass wide of Howard Radford into his own net. Things could have been worse. Harry's attempted back-heeled pass stuck between his own legs almost on the goal line but, luckily, Radford managed to clear it. Rovers couldn't sustain their winning streak against Barnsley, scoring three, including Geoff Bradford's 100th for the club, but conceding four, although Pat Kavanagh thought Barnsley's winner offside and that Ward had a goal unjustly disallowed 30 seconds from the whistle. On 26 November, the goal rush reached its height when 23,728 at Eastville were treated to seven goals without reply against Middlesbrough, Harry spending most of the closing minutes deep in Middlesbrough territory looking for his annual goal. Bristol City were also on a roll, occupying first place with Rovers a point behind them in second.

Not every Rovers' supporter was delighted by the excitement their all-out attacking policy was generating. Pat Kavanagh, responding to the Rovers' faithful's concerns that the team was conceding too many goals, pointed out that such a policy inevitably meant that the amount of defensive cover would be reduced. He believed that the general defensive plan had been disrupted by this, but also because Ian Muir who had stood in for Ray Warren, out with a pulled muscle for five weeks, was a more forward-thinking centre-half 'in the Scottish style' and wasn't as 'stay-at-home' as Warren, who would focus on 'policing his own territory' while the other defenders would position themselves either side.

Rovers, for various reasons, were about to have another difficult, disappointing December. The defence tightened up, but the goals dried up too. The month opened with a defeat by Notts County, who overpowered the Rovers' defence forcing them into a number of errors. Harry was guilty of not making a simple clearance on the half hour which gave Notts County their second. Despite Rovers pulling the score back to 2-2 in the first half, the home side scored another three to win 5-2. Against West Ham on 10 December, a 'promotion performance' by Rovers secured a 1-1 draw, in which Harry joined the attack in the final 15 minutes and 'to the astonishment of the crowd started putting over immaculate crosses'. The defence could do nothing to prevent West Ham's freak equaliser when a hopeful shot was caught by the wind and blown in. It wasn't only the wind which blew up a storm; West Ham's tough play led to five more Rovers' men joining the injury list. Josser Watling was concussed and played part of the game in a daze and – a rarity for those times – Noel Cantwell was sent off for a foul on Jackie Pitt. When Pitt was hurt a second time the referee called both teams together in the centre circle to give them a talking to, though Pat Kavanagh thought the official was over-reacting. Jackie Pitt might have seen it differently. Rovers lost two of their three games over the Christmas period and won only two of their seven December outings.

The FA Cup was, once again, to steal the show in Rovers' season, because they had drawn a home tie against the glamour team of the day, the 'Busby Babes' of Manchester United. Harry was not intimidated by United's reputation. In an interview with the *Weekend Mail* entitled 'We've Done It Before – We'll Do It Again' he spelled out why he believed Rovers had a realistic chance of upsetting the form book. 'We're used to beating top teams in the Cup,' he said, reminding readers of the two epic games against Newcastle in 1951. Rovers' greatest asset was that they were 'essentially a family team, depending basically on local talent that we can develop up to a national footballing standard'. This gave them two big advantages. 'First, because of the 'home' aspect of the team we get an even greater spur than most teams from playing before our own fans on our own ground. Our second big advantage comes from so many of our players having been together for five years or more. We know each other's play inside out – even the supposedly 'unexpected' moves.' And there was always the 'Eastville roar'.

Did Rovers have any special plans to beat United? Harry was hardly going to reveal all Rovers' secrets, but he pointed out proudly that there were things which Rovers shared with their more-feted opponents: 'Well, for a start, our approach to the match will be based on the same kind of on-the-carpet football as theirs – combined with as much strength and determination as the boys can muster'. Rovers, he said, would not be trying to beat United at their own game, as this was their usual style of play. However, Harry concluded with a warning that the Cup run must come to an end at some point and that Rovers must not be distracted from their greatest ambition, which was not to win the Cup, but to join Manchester United in the top league. The accompanying picture was captioned: 'He has a baby daughter not quite three months old, but hopes to produce a son one day – just for Rovers' benefit'.

Despite the woeful festive form, there were some reasons for optimism. New Year's Eve's home encounter with Sheffield Wednesday who had torn Rovers apart earlier in the season turned the tables on the League leaders, Rovers fighting back after conceding an early goal from Quixall to win 4-2. Ron Nicholls, the young Gloucestershire County cricketer, made his league debut in goal and teenager Alfie Biggs scored twice. During the half-time interval there was a collection for Harry, George Petherbridge, Howard Radford and Barry Watkins who had all qualified for a benefit. The Eastville pitch was once again heavy – even the home defence was leaden-footed in the mud – but the opinion was that the conditions would give Rovers yet another advantage.

Rovers' fans were to enjoy an extra, belated New Year celebration. What took place on the 7 January 1956 sent shockwaves around English football and has justifiably been enshrined in Rovers' folklore. Sir Stanley Rous, Chairman of the FA and other football luminaries, as well as 35,872 people, mostly frenzied gasheads, witnessed the 10-1 favourites United being 'publicly spanked' and 'given a football lesson' by 150-1 outsiders Rovers. Desmond 'The Man in the Brown Bowler' Hackett, one of the most famous and flamboyant sport writers in the country declared: 'Manchester United were not just beaten – they were paralysed. It could have been 8-0. In every position this £110 Bristol outfit with the million dollar touch of class was the better.' Midfield prodigy and England star Duncan Edwards was injured, so he did not play, but United fielded a strong side: Ray Wood in goal; Bill Foulkes and Roger Byrne who were England international full-backs; Eddie Colman, Mark Jones and Jeff Whitefoot; and a forward line of Johnny Berry, John Doherty, Tommy Taylor, Dennis Viollet and David Pegg, who would play their part in winning the First Division Championship that summer. Along with Edwards, five of those men (Byrne, Colman, Jones, Pegg and Taylor) lost their lives two years later in the Munich Air Disaster.

As Ron Nicholls kept a clean sheet, hurling himself at anything sent his way, 19-year-old Lance Corporal Alfie Biggs stunned United by scoring Rovers' first on 19 minutes, to, Hackett claimed, roars of 'Make him a General'. United, Hackett said, committed the cardinal sin of

'World class' Harry helps to keep Manchester United out in Rovers' famous Cup giant-killing on 7 January 1956

underestimating their opponents. The visitors 'could not think of any other plan beyond short square-passes which either stuck in the mud or were cut off by men with an appetite for action'.

Rovers' wingers, George Petherbridge '5ft 4 inches of genius and impudence' and Peter Hooper ran rings round Foulkes and Byrne, 'If Byrne is England's best, ' Hackett observed, 'then on this showing Bristol right-back Harry Bamford must be world class'. Captain Byrne, usually a cultured and assured player, rather lost his cool. He had his name taken for a foul on Jackie Pitt and gave away a penalty for handball. Byrne believed he had equalized when Rovers were 1-0 up, but had wrongly thought the referee had indicated a free kick rather than an indirect free kick and shot straight into the net. His 'goal' was naturally disallowed. Barrie Meyer made it 2-0 in the second half, Biggs adding the third before Bradford's penalty conversion set the finishing touch to a famous victory.

But Rovers, as Harry had counselled, had to put the euphoria quickly behind them. Pat Kavanagh in his a comment piece 'The Great Promotion Struggle', highlighted exactly what both Rovers and City, each on 29 points from 25 games, had still to do, given that only nine points separated the 20 teams. 54 points, he reckoned, the total that had seen Birmingham City and Luton Town go up the previous season, was the target. Promotion form was to win your home games and draw away. On paper, Kavanagh argued, Rovers had a better chance than their neighbours because they had nine remaining home games to City's eight. One of those home games was, however, the Bristol derby, a 'four point needle match'. Although erratic, Rovers were three points better off than a year ago. The favourite to win the Second Division was Sheffield Wednesday, two points in front, albeit having played an extra match, with the best defensive record in the top half of the table.

In the next two games Rovers got the required three points, drawing away against Nottingham Forest and beating bottom of the table Hull City 4-2 with a hat-trick from Bradford, having fought back from two goals down. The FA Cup again interrupted their League progress, a 1-1 draw against Doncaster Rovers quickly followed by a replay away under the novelty of floodlights. Rovers were defeated by the only goal of the game in the 87th minute, but a far bigger loss was the serious injury sustained by Geoff Bradford, who had scored 26 goals in 28 League and Cup games. While Bradford waited in a Clifton nursing home for an operation on his knee, Bert Tann ruled out any venture into the transfer market. One Rovers' fan wrote to the *Pink 'Un* to say that he would gladly personally contribute £5 towards buying a centre-forward and others would too, but Tann thought Rovers adequately covered in all departments, a belief which wasn't shaken even when Alfie Biggs was injured playing for the Army. Rovers' results were highly inconsistent, as the team began to rely on 'Tann's Babes' for goals. The four-pointer against Bristol City on 3 March ended in a bitter 3-0 defeat, after City took control in the second half, John Atyeo scoring twice. For the second goal, Atyeo's shot bounced off Harry high into the air and Jimmy Rogers rushed in to head the ball past Nicholls, but Harry also made two important clearances, tried, in partnership with Pitt to get the attack going and had the best chance of the second half, moving upfield to take a pass from Petherbridge and send in a quick shot which went narrowly wide of the post.

The injuries piled up. In acting skipper Jackie Pitt's absence from a dislocated shoulder sustained in training, Harry, as captain, led the Rovers out on an Upton Park pitch almost devoid of grass to lose 2-1 to West Ham, thanks to what Rovers felt was a highly unjust penalty. By the middle of March, Rovers had slipped to fifth, but they were still in with a chance, largely thanks to the young Dai Ward's goals. All three of Rovers' Easter games were against sides battling against relegation, Plymouth Argyle twice and Rotherham United. All were hard games – but although Rovers narrowly did the double over Plymouth, they suffered a shock defeat against Rotherham 4-1, Ian Wilson, the Rotherham outside-left, scoring a hat-trick in the second half.

Even Harry resorted to booting the ball straight out into the terraces rather than take any chances as the nerves set in. He said of the game, in the Harry Bamford Story, that it was an occasion when 'the spirit was lacking' in the second half. 'Five defenders found themselves facing seven attackers. That was asking for trouble and we got it. Those of you who were at the match will recall the way the Rotherham wing-halves were able to bring the ball upfield all too often unchallenged.' Harry had no truck with those who argued that playing three games over Easter and at Christmas affected promotion too much and worked against those with fewer resources, claiming that 'if a footballer has prepared and trained for these high peaks and has spent his time off the field quietly, there is no real hardship in playing three games in such a short period. A great deal rests with the individual.'

However, Rovers still kept themselves in the promotion chase, on 7 April scraping a 1-0 win over Middlesbrough thanks to Ward's seventh goal in six games which put them second on 46 points behind clear leaders Sheffield Wednesday on 51. Their two nearest challengers, Leeds and Nottingham Forest, had games in hand.

Unaccountably, only 15,505 came to Eastville on 14 April to see Rovers maintain their run with a 2-0 win over Notts County. Everything now depended on the last two tough matches against fellow promotion challengers Leeds and Liverpool. Harry explained why the Leeds game was Bristol Rovers' most important ever:

'Seldom has soccer seen such a struggle as the one taking place in the dying weeks of this season at the top of the second division. You could call it the yo-yo division for a misplaced pass, or a shot inches the wrong side of the post can send a team bouncing up and down the table.

'For the old 'uns – and at 36 I am in that category – it possibly represents our last chance of realising every player's ambition to appear regularly against the top men in the sport.'

Harry pointed out that, in a team depleted by injury, the key to Rovers' success in these games rested on the shoulders of the youngsters drafted in. 'They need to take as their inspiration our young Welsh-born inside-forward Dai Ward. For sheer technical skill Dai is still behind some of the others but he more than makes up for this by playing flat out for the full ninety minutes.'

But Rovers' tried and tested formula was vitally important. Since Bert Tann had joined the club, Harry went on, 'our game has been based on a solid, balanced defence in which all eleven men had a part to play. We play to a well-tried system that when an opponent has possession of the ball we are all defenders. The forwards have to skate back to make a challenge and by tackling, recovering and going into the tackle again, rob or harry the other attack into making errors. Equally, our task in defence is to close the gaps in possession and work the ball through to start a Rovers' attack. Put down this way in a few paragraphs it seems simple enough but to play it properly demands 100 per cent match-fitness, ability and above all determination.'

Harry was also anxious to stress the impact of the weight of expectations on all footballers. 'The other night on TV Sheffield Wednesday's skipper Redfern Froggatt said how much easier his side are finding it to play away from home just now. So, too, are Bristol Rovers. Our crowd at Eastville is very tense. They are so earnest in their desire to see us go up and so critical of error that a player can be put right off his normal game. You try something, it fails. To a roar of "Get rid of it" you try it again, with perhaps another failure. On the third occasion the temptation just to boot the ball away from you is so strong that you are forced to do the wrong thing. I know, because it has happened to me. Away from home the problem disappears. The crowd is not half as interested in what you are doing, unless you happen to be taking the ball away from the local idol. The result is you can relax mentally and settle down to thinking and play constructively. I believe it is more helpful to give a good pass instead of belting the ball down the middle where it has more than a 50-50 chance of being collected by an opposing defender. Sometimes I run into trouble but it's usually a calculated risk.'

The Leeds United team which effectively stood between Rovers and promotion had the best home record in the League, having only lost one game. This crucial fixture attracted a remarkable crowd to Elland Road on 21 April of 49,274, the record League crowd Rovers have ever played in front of before or since. Rovers had a dream start, Dai Ward scoring once again, this time after only two minutes. But Leeds soon fought back, their magisterial centre-half/centre-forward, Welsh international John Charles, another 'gentle giant', scoring the equaliser with his head

30 April 1956: Captain Harry is handed the Gloucestershire Senior Professional Cup after Rovers' 1-0 victory over Bristol City

Harry's four Gloucestershire Senior Cup winner's medal

Harry's souvenir lapel badge from the match in Jersey to commemorate Liberation Day

and making the second for Jack Overfield in the 28th minute. Harry stayed cool throughout in the cup-final like atmosphere, and there was no further addition to Leeds' tally, or, sadly, to Rovers', who lost 2-1 and saw their hopes evaporate. The final league match, at home, ended in a defeat by the same score line, Liverpool's victory being sealed with a goal from Geoff Twentyman, father of the future Rovers' defender and broadcaster of the same name, and leaving Rovers to finish sixth, not consoled by attaining their highest final position so far in the Division.

The disappointment for both Bristol clubs manifested itself in the lowest-ever attendance for the Gloucestershire Cup Final since the war (apart from a 1947 replay) 11,952, on 30 April at Ashton Gate. Harry, who captained the side which won 1-0, did not allow it to affect his performance, the *Evening World* noting approvingly: 'The most polished, and certainly the calmest player, was the Rovers' evergreen Harry Bamford. He treated the game, indeed I believe he does even the most vital encounter, with cold academic detachment.' In the accompanying photograph, a mud-spattered Harry received the Gloucestershire Football Association Professional Cup, and his fourth and final winners' medal in the competition from the president of the GFA Mr. J. Kennedy.

Harry had no time to brood on what might have been, Rovers flying out to St. Helier in Jersey for the second year running to play against Cardiff City from Whitchurch airfield to commemorate Liberation Day on 8 May. A headed goal from John McIlvenny gave them the victory. And once again, he trained for most of the close season, determined to be at his fittest for the new campaign.

CHAPTER 12

'Just Like Harry of the Old Days'

While Bristol Rovers' marquee at Weston was being destroyed by a gale on 29 July 1956, Harry was warm and dry in Taunton, preparing to teach on the first full week's residential soccer course promoted by the Somerset County Football Association's Youth section at Queens College. Among his papers survives the list of the 46 boys who were accepted, some of whom went on to have professional and semi-professional careers in football. Harry was joined by Peter Coombes, a schoolmaster who later taught PE and Music at Withywood School and was on Rovers' books. John Gummow, Rovers' secretary, proudly explained to the *Evening World* that the Rovers' qualified coaches were now more fully occupied than at any other time in the club's history, citing Harry and Coombes as prime examples. During the winter, Gummow said, with the assistance of Rovers' sound film projector, the coaching scheme was being pressed forward throughout a large area of the West Country.

Rovers' fourth season in the Second Division began in the wettest August since 1917 and proved to be a fraught one for their defence which conceded 67 goals, twice letting in seven. Speaking at the end of the season, Bert Tann was adamant that the responsibility could not be laid at the door of 36-year-old veterans Harry Bamford and Jackie Pitt. The *Pink 'Un*'s season round-up agreed with him: 'they had a few patchy games, but their fine ball play was still in evidence and they again acquitted themselves with great credit to show just how great club-men they are. Without their skill and endeavour, the Rovers might well have been in serious difficulties.' Harry had now been at Rovers long enough

Serious students: Harry and Pete Coombes prepare to coach in Taunton. Harry is wearing his FA coach's badge

Harry plays the banjo on the Christmas cover of Soccer Star

to earn his second benefit in the game against Sheffield Wednesday on 6 October for which he was awarded the maximum payment of £750.

Although Harry and Jackie Pitt were undoubtedly slowing down and could get caught out if they ventured too far upfield, Rovers could not yet do without them; both missed only three League games apiece. Instead, the left flank was giving Bert Tann problems. Frank Allcock was recuperating in a Clifton nursing home after an operation on the knee injury which would end his Rovers' career just when he was hitting his peak. Leslie Edwards, his replacement, injured his ankle in the sixth game of the season against Huddersfield and young David Lawrence was forced to make his League debut against Middlesbrough on 8 September in a 3-2 defeat engineered by the prolific goal-scorer and future brilliant and controversial football manager Brian Clough. Lawrence's inexperience was exposed and Tann dropped him after he was given a torrid time by City's winger David Smith in the Bristol derby which Rovers lost 5-3. When Edwards was again injured in November, Bert Tann made one of his inspired positional switches to fill the void. Even when Josser Watling had been a regular at left-wing in the Rovers' attack, Tann had told Pat Kavanagh that he had a hunch that he would make a 'first-class back'. After a few outings at left-back for the Reserves, Josser was drafted into that position against Swansea on 10 November where he 'was an outstanding success' against Welsh international Cliff Jones, although he was rarely used again this season. When Edwards, Watling and Lawrence were all unfit on 19 January, another inexperienced debutant, Cecil Steeds, was at left-back as Rovers were crushed 7-2 by Leicester City. Centre-half Ian Muir became the fifth Rovers' player to occupy the berth in December.

Despite all the later praise for the 'Old Faithfuls', Harry's game suffered as he was drawn out of position while covering for less experienced full-back partners. By October when Edwards returned and the defensive line-up became more settled, there was a significant improvement in his form. Against Barnsley on 13 October, Harry had a battle of wits with John McCann. 'For half an hour the clever winger tricked Big Harry on the inside and outside', until Harry got his measure and 'took the ball off his opponent's toe again and again with delightfully judged tackles and interceptions'. Against Rotherham on 27 October, in one of many tussles with outside-left Keith Bambridge, Harry coolly rested his foot on the ball as it lay against the corner flag to much amusement in the crowd.

And then came December. Rovers lost four out of their seven games as part of their now traditional slump and also lost the first two League games in January 1957. The local papers dubbed it 'crazy Christmas' when in the three matches between 22 December and Boxing Day, Rovers beat Doncaster Rovers 6-1, lost 7-2 to strugglers Bury away, then thumped them 6-1 at Eastville the next day. Not many people actually saw Rovers' goals against Doncaster, which included a quick-fire, five-minute hat-trick from Dai Ward, even if they made it to Eastville, because of the thick fog which kept the attendance down to 12,186 and settled over the pitch like an 'opaque white blanket'. The Christmas Day humiliation by Bury was one of those nightmare games where everything went wrong. Ron Nicholls punched three shots into his own net and Harry was responsible for mistakes which led to two goals. In the return on Boxing Day the tables were turned. It had been a white Christmas at Eastville, which the players had missed while they were up North, only for it to thaw the next day and leave the pitch a mud bath. Although many struggled in the conditions, Harry 'did not put a foot wrong'. He 'might have been playing on Wembley's immaculate carpet, such was the delicacy and finesse he displayed, even under pressure'.

Harry appeared on the Christmas cover of the weekly football magazine *Soccer Star*, rather bizarrely playing the banjo and singing, though this was the over-imaginative, and perhaps ironic, invention of a cartoonist who had drawn him doing so under a photo of his face. The caption read: 'Getting you in the Festive Mood is Harry Bamford, Bristol Rovers' jovial right-back, seen below in a gay mood (with the help of our artist). Bristol-born Harry keeps valuable racing pigeons as a hobby – but it's turkey, not pigeon, for Xmas Dinner.'

There was some New Year cheer when Rovers beat First Division Hull City 4-3 in a thrilling cup tie in which Harry and Les Edwards played a large part in just about repelling Hull's second-half onslaught. A bravura display by the sublime Tom Finney for First Division Preston cut Rovers cup campaign short in the Fourth Round, though the 'Preston plumber' did miss a penalty.

Unusually, Harry missed the 2-0 defeat by Middlesbrough at Eastville on 12 January when Rovers were forced to field three reserves in their defence. He was originally reported as being confined to bed with a heavy cold and Ian Muir stood in for him. A throwaway comment in the *Evening World* the next week revealed something which had never been publicly mentioned before: 'Harry Bamford, out last week with a recurrence of his war-time malaria, back now in training'. We know that Harry had said in a past interview that he had nearly died when he was serving in the Far East, but not what had made him so ill. A family member recalls that everyone knew that Harry's younger brother Alan had had malaria, but not Harry. Assuming that the paper had got the facts straight, it could be that Harry had considered he was cured, or that he preferred to keep this knowledge to himself in the early part of his career in case it cast doubts on his long-term fitness. Malarial parasites can remain dormant in the liver and the disease can recur, but given Harry's excellent physical condition and his general good health this may have been a one-off event. If he had kept this information quiet, Rovers could hardly complain.

On 19 January, Harry was back in the team but had a poor game, like every other Rovers' player on the pitch that day, against eventual runaway League winners Leicester City alongside the unfortunate Cecil Steeds who was 'passed time and time again' by speedy winger John Wright. But the 7-2 defeat was Rovers' last in the League for the next two months. Harry and Jackie Pitt both showed they had lost none of their fire or grit, digging deep to inspire Rovers' revival. In the drawn Bristol derby on 2 February, Pitt was sent off for fighting with City's Ernie Peacock, both of the combatants having to be attended to by their trainers before they left the pitch arm-in-arm. Harry aggravated a pulled chest muscle after ten minutes in a bruising encounter against Barnsley on 23 February in which even the referee was injured, but carried on, although he was clearly in some pain. Brushing aside suggestions that he should not come out for the second half, he was given a pain-killing injection which enabled him to help secure a 1-1 draw. He left the field at the end in obvious discomfort and missed the next two matches.

Geoff Bradford had enjoyed several successful outings at right-back in the Reserves where he was seeking to regain his confidence following his second injury, and stood in for Harry in the first team's 4-2 win against Rotherham. But, quite rightly, Bert Tann decided he needed Bradford to score goals, not keep them out. Once he had recovered from his chest injury, Harry seemed to become stronger. The *Post*'s John Coe reflected after Rovers narrowly lost to Lincoln City on 16 March where 'the big man in the Rovers' defence now emerged as a giant', repeatedly covering for goalkeeper Ron Nicholls and kicking off the line: 'Now more than ever, must Rovers' manager Mr. Bert Tann, wonder where he is going eventually to find a replacement for this sterling character.'

Rovers, maddeningly inconsistent over Easter, eventually finished in ninth position, disgruntled supporters writing to the local papers to criticise what they saw as a slavish adherence to the 'no buy no sell' policy which meant that untried youngsters had to be drafted in rather than experienced replacements being bought. Although Leicester won the Second Division title by a handsome margin, the second place was up for grabs for a long time and supporters felt that Rovers should have been spending some money to enable the team to occupy it. Instead, sensationally, their exciting forward Dai Ward whose relationship with Bert Tann had become strained, was placed on the transfer list for £12,000. However, by the start of the next season Tann announced that 'all was forgiven and forgotten' and that Ward had returned to the fold. Rovers, said their manager, were starting the new campaign with one of their strongest squads ever, full of young, local talent and, with the retirement of Ray Warren, containing only two 'old stagers' in Harry and Jackie Pitt. One of the most important new signings was experienced 27-year-old full-back Brian Doyle who had played for Stoke and Exeter City. Although Doyle partnered Harry at left-back in the Rovers' trial game, Josser Watling and Harry would play the first 23 League games in tandem, with Doyle turning out for the Reserves. After the first few matches, particularly the decisive 5-2 win against Derby County on 26 August in which, according to Pat Kavanagh, he was 'cool and clever, distributing the ball with great skill, Watling was 'now looking every inch a full-back and a possible replacement for Harry Bamford when the veteran finally retires from the game'.

Harry's involvement in local youth coaching showed no signs of diminishing. In April he had attended the Senior Six-a-side Soccer Tournament organised by the Bristol and District Federation of Boys' Clubs at Monks Park, where he must have been delighted to see his old school side St. Silas win their final 7-1. He presented the senior trophy to Douglas Carrington, their captain, as well as the junior trophy to the Bristol Five team from St. George. At some point he also began working as a football coach in a school in Clifton in the afternoon after training.

As the 1957-58 season got underway, it soon became apparent that the Rovers' right flank had become even more vulnerable to pace. Harry and Jackie Pitt were frequently in trouble against the fast and tricky Malcolm Musgrove on 31 August and two of the three goals in Billy Dare's hat-trick which gave West Ham a 3-2 win came from crosses they failed to cut out. 'Bathonian' got out his pen again to complain to the *Pink 'Un* that opponents knew the Rovers' defence was slow and planned accordingly. Tann's solution was to replace Pitt with Graham Ricketts for the next game against Derby County, in which Ray Mabbutt, father of future Rovers' player Gary, made his League debut replacing Geoff Bradford. Rovers lost 2-1, but Harry, captaining the side, had a better game, though there was an extraordinary ending to the match, the referee blowing his whistle and the players trooping off, only to be recalled to play another minute.

In the awful Rovers' performance at Sheffield United on 7 September, where they lost 2-0, Harry put the ball into his own net after 13 minutes when attempting to head it back to Ron Nicholls, and the side 'looked like a set of individuals drifting aimlessly across the pitch'. This prompted Tann to recall his more experienced men: Pitt, George Petherbridge and Peter Sampson, perhaps one of Rovers' most underrated players.

The 'old' defensive line-up of Harry, Watling, Pitt, Hale and Sampson steadied the ship temporarily with three straight wins, including a welcome first clean sheet of the season against Blackburn Rovers.

But the Rovers' manager had to look towards the long-term. In the two defeats which ended October, both by two goals without reply against Cardiff City and Liverpool, Harry and Jackie Pitt were caught out of position too many times and Watling and Sampson had their work cut out trying to plug the gaps they left. When Pitt was dropped to be replaced by Norman Sykes who acquitted himself well, Harry reaped the benefit of Sykes' speed. Tann was particularly pleased by the defensive performance which earned a hard-fought 1-0 win against his old club Charlton Athletic. 'Our defence today,' he enthused, 'played just like Charlton used to, with every man running into position to cover a colleague and with scoring chances by the opposition cut to almost nil.' 'Bathonian' was also inspired by Rovers' dogged resistance to compose yet another missive to the *Pink 'Un*, in which he gave most of the credit to one man, with an honourable mention for another:

'And how our defence played, especially during that final, desperate period when Charlton threw everything into attack. Splendidly led by Harry Bamford they presented a solid front to all the visitors could do.

'I have often criticised Harry Bamford for being somewhat dilatory in his clearances, but his displays, both against Middlesbrough and Charlton, were without blemish. In fact, just like the Harry of the old days. As for John Watling he is one of the great successes of the season. He improves in every match and by now ranks with the best left-backs in the Second Division.'

Rovers had yet another dire December. A humiliating 7-0 defeat by Grimsby Town on the 14th in which the defence was reduced to a 'shambles' was not the last League appearance for Jack Pitt in a Rovers' shirt, as he played once more, against Ipswich on 1 February, but it effectively signalled that his days as a first team player were more or less over. As injuries piled up, Paddy Hale was switched to left-back for two games, one of which, a 3-0 win against Swansea, was Rovers' lone victory in December, but in the second the Rovers' defence was 'cut to ribbons' by a swiftly-moving West Ham attack' and was 'as wide open as a barn door'. 20 goals had been shipped in the last five matches. Bert Tann told the papers that he had seven scouts out urgently looking for 'a full-back or two and a left-winger'.

Thankfully, the FA Cup was once more about to set Rovers' faltering season alight. The campaign began with a morale-boosting 5-0 rout of Midlands League Mansfield Town on 4 January, whose player-manager Charlie Mitten was so 'buttoned up' by Harry that the Eastville faithful cheered loudly on the few occasions Mitten managed to get by him. When the Fourth Round tie on 25 January against First Division Burnley, unbeaten in 30 games, was jeopardised by a three-inch fall of snow which thawed, a gang of players, club employees and volunteers made such a 'superhuman effort' to mop up the deep pools on the pitch with blankets and squeegees so that there was no surface water left. The game was saved from postponement a mere hour before kick off. The two sides still 'slid and slithered' on a treacherous surface, Hale giving Rovers the lead until Burnley went ahead after scoring two deflected goals in two minutes. After an own goal by Leslie Shannon gifted them an equaliser, Rovers were pressed back in defence but both Harry and Josser Watling kept their heads, continuing to play the ball out and distribute it constructively, in contrast to the wild clearances of Sykes and Sampson on the left. After the match, the Fifth Round draw thrillingly paired Bristol City and Rovers – but Rovers had to get past Burnley in their replay first.

'Eleven heroes' was how the *Evening World* paid tribute to the Rovers' men who pulled off a remarkable giant-killing 3-2 victory on 28 January watched by 40,813, including many from Bristol. Bert Tann gambled, successfully, on bringing back Jackie Pitt, hoping that his 'vast experience would make up for the slowness made inevitable' by his years. Although initially both Pitt and Harry were out-paced by Burnley's Cheeseborough-Pilkington left wing combination, the two old comrades sorted matters out and blotted them entirely from the game in the second half, joining forces with their wing-halves in a series of fierce attacks. In the 74th minute, Dai Ward equalised to make it 2-2, before scoring the winner ten minutes from time.

As Rovers' away League match against Notts County was cancelled because of a waterlogged pitch, they did not participate in the country-wide minute's silence for the eight members of the Manchester United team who tragically lost their lives, along with 13 others, when their aeroplane crashed at Munich's Riem airport on the way back from a European Cup-tie. A collection for the dependents' fund was made among Rovers fans queuing for tickets at All Hallows Hall in Easton for their Fifth Round Cup-tie against the City on 15 February, which the local papers rated as 'The Best and Most Exciting Derby Ever'. After a shock City goal in the fourth minute, Rovers led 3-1 courtesy of Meyer, Sykes and Ward, before a City fight-back in the second half made it all square. Geoff Bradford got the winner in the 83rd minute – offside, according to the City fans who made up the majority of the 39,126 crowd. Ron Nicholls saved a penalty because Josser Watling took him to one side and told him to dive to his right where John Watkins always put his spot-kicks.

The Cup run came to an end in the quarter-finals with a 3-1 defeat by Fulham in front of 42,000, Norman Sykes understandably finding the task of subduing England's Johnny Haynes too onerous. After their opponents scored twice in the first 13 minutes, Rovers struggled to get back in the game, especially when Josser Watling was injured and finished the match as a passenger on the left-wing. However, the upswing in Rovers' League form continued, so much so that until Easter (from when Rovers did not win another match), there was still an outside chance of promotion and, if not, 'talent money' for finishing in the top four. Harry stood out in this purple patch. Even in Rovers' dreadful showing in the Gloucestershire Senior Cup, which they lost 4-1, he gave a 'model display'. Pat Kavanagh in the Bristol Rovers' supporters' Club Year Book did not hesitate to pick Harry as the Rovers' Man of the season, the only ever-present, ever-consistent and, with his constructive play, 'always a joy to watch'.

Since he reached the age of 32, Harry had been referred to as a veteran. Six years on in August 1958, aged 38, he was about to start his 14th

1 March 1958: Ron Nicholls and Harry Bamford fail to stop Stevens scoring Fulham's third goal in the match which put an end to Rovers' thrilling Cup run

season for Rovers and occupy his usual position in the opener against Leyton Orient at Brisbane Road. Some familiar faces were absent from the Rovers' line up but others made surprise returns. Jackie Pitt had retired after 466 League appearances to take charge of Rovers' Colts team. 21-year-old Bristolian Norman Sykes replaced Pitt at inside-left, while David Pyle, also 21, took over at centre-half from Paddy Hale. Gloucestershire cricketers Barrie Meyer and Ron Nicholls' refusal to cut their cricket season short by a month to take part in the whole of Rovers' pre-season training had led to both being transferred. Nicholls' unexpected departure and an injury to young Malcolm Norman created a goalkeeping crisis which led to a recall for Howard Radford. George Petherbridge was also back for his first League game since February.

Harry still had every confidence that he was fit and capable enough to hold down a regular first team place. When asked in April by one of the senior Rovers' officials how long it would be before he retired, he was quick to scotch any idea that any announcement might be imminent: 'Oh, not yet. I think I've got another three years' football at least in me'. But it was more than likely that Bert Tann would begin gradually bedding in Harry's successor as the season went on. Even though Josser Watling was fit, Brian Doyle had partnered Harry at left-back for several matches towards last season's end. Tann had no intention of Doyle replacing Watling, who had shown he shared something of Harry's talent for clever distribution, but was probably taking the opportunity to ready Doyle for some outings at right-back when the time was right.

Violet and Harry had learned they were expecting their second child that summer. The first-floor club flat in Montpelier was hardly ideal for their growing toddler Hilary, let alone two children. The Bamfords could have asked Rovers to move them, but as players lost their club accommodation once they retired, Harry had decided to provide long-term security for his family by buying their own home. He had enough life savings to purchase outright a semi-detached house in Broomhill in Brislington on one of the new estates which were springing up in the Bristol suburbs. The local papers were full of advertisements for these properties, a semi-detached costing around £1,600.

Harry had also continued building up his coaching qualifications and experience, missing the start of training because he was again at Lilleshall and afterwards working with Peter Coombes on another Somerset County FA Youth section residential course in Taunton. A photograph in the paper showed the two demonstrating the art of defensive tackling in front of their eager students. As mentioned earlier, at some point Harry had begun regularly coaching football in a private school in Clifton, after previously coaching boys at Pinehursts in Swindon. Clark's Grammar School had two sites, one in Alma Road and the other in Pembroke Road. Photographs in the family archives show Harry on the stage in what appears to be the school hall in Alma Road, wearing his FA coach's badge while supervising a drill and demonstrating how to chest the ball down. In another he is coaching boys probably on the nearby Bristol Downs, which served as Clark's playing fields. One newspaper article commented that Harry had developed a 'passion' for youth coaching

Coaching boys at Clark's Grammar School in Clifton

and that rather than sitting at home with his feet up after training he chose to spend his afternoons working in a school doing something he loved. Harry had patience in abundance and a quiet, yet firm authority ideal for coaching schoolboys. As his notes from one of his training courses counselled: 'The Coach – May have reputation. Must live up to it. Boys soon find weaknesses.'

Rovers' made a winning start to the 1958-59 season. During the 3-1 defeat of Leyton Orient, Harry had to leave the field for a time to have three stitches inserted in a cut over his right eye while Geoff Bradford covered for him. The *Pink 'Un* had introduced the practice of giving ratings to individual players and Harry earned a seven, only bettered by Radford with an eight, in what was deemed an excellent defensive display. In their first ever visit to Bristol, sweltering in fierce sunshine, Scunthorpe were easily beaten 4-0 with the two star Rovers' performers George Petherbridge and 'still wearing a plaster over the eye injury of the week before, Harry Bamford'. 'He has always been known as an immaculate passer of the ball,' wrote Pat Kavanagh, 'but I have never seen him better than he was in this game.' Derby County on 3 September proved tougher opponents, going 3-0 up before half-time. Although Rovers staged a second half fight-back, they disappointingly lost 3-2; Harry, Josser Watling and Howard Radford all sustained injuries. Harry pulled a muscle in the calf of his right leg just before the interval and was obviously in difficulties for the rest of the game, not being able to attempt any long kicking, though he did his job well enough to earn another seven rating.

Harry's pulled muscle would normally have kept him out for two games, but, even though he quickly returned to fitness, stand-in Brian Doyle, who had a magnificent game in the 0-0 draw with Fulham, continued at right back and Harry found himself in the Reserves for only the 11th time since he first signed for Rovers in August 1946. The Rovers' Reserve team was struggling, close to the bottom of the Combination League table. On 17 September they lost 4-1 to Ipswich Town, who fielded five first-teamers, despite the defence being 'well-marshalled' by Harry Bamford and with Paddy Hale's experience at

Harry training at Eastville

centre-half. Bert Tann in his regular column in the *Green 'Un* warned against writing Harry off too soon, describing him as 'Still fit, as gifted as ever, and so keen that he puts some of his younger fellow professionals to shame, he is far from finished… In fact he has rammed criticisms down the throats of some people who have written him off.'

Tann explained that the form of Brian Doyle in recent games had been responsible for the change, but that Harry had accepted it with his customary grace and his dry wit. Tann pointed out to people that Harry was 'quite a humorist'. 'When I asked him if he was fit for the game on Wednesday, his reply was: "I was fit last Saturday."' Elsewhere Tann put matters more bluntly: 'There is a lot of good football left in Harry, and he is really worth his place in the team, but Brian Doyle is the younger man and I have left him in because the future seems to rest with him'. In the short term, Rovers seemed to manage well without Harry, having their best start in the Second Division, 16 points from 12 games, some of their luckier fans enjoying sitting in the new £60,000 stand, which one described as like 'watching football from a circle cinema seat'.

Meanwhile, Harry, ever the professional, was trying his hardest to improve the Reserves. A crowd of 5,289 came to Eastville to watch Arsenal Reserves give the Rovers a football masterclass, Harry inadvertently scoring Arsenal's last and eighth goal when diving full-length to head out, only for the ball to fly straight into the net. There was a satisfying 2-0 win against Bristol City in which Harry was 'prominent'. Ray Bean, then a young player, has never forgotten meeting Harry when he travelled as 12th man with the Reserves to the Valley to play Charlton Athletic on 18 October. Ray was sitting awkwardly on his own, when Harry came over to talk to him, putting him at his ease, asking him about his career while being keen to stress that not all budding footballers would make the grade. When Ray told him that he was an apprentice plumber, Harry was very approving. The match report commented: 'While his colleague struggled, the experienced Bamford, despite being out-paced by winger Kinsey, never seemed unduly worried. His coolness paid off when, during the second half, he headed away a certain goal from under the bar'.

All smiles at the Douglas training ground, Kingswood. L-R Jack Pitt, Harry, George Petherbridge and Bryan Bush

As Bert Tann remarked, Harry 'will keep playing for whichever side he is selected for with the same high sense of club spirit he has always shown... He will fight as hard to get back into the League side as any other man on the staff.'

CHAPTER 13

'A Part of Bristol Rovers Died With Him'

Howard Radford looked at his watch. He was at Clark's Grammar School in Clifton on Tuesday 28 October, waiting for Harry Bamford to arrive to begin their coaching session with the boys. And, very unusually, Harry was late. As time ticked on Howard began to feel uneasy, as it was so unlike his reliable team mate and friend to let anyone down.

Harry had finished training at Eastville that morning and gone home to eat lunch with his family. He and Violet were temporarily living in Moor Street in St. Philip's Marsh with his parents while their new house in Brislington was being finished. Then he had climbed on the Vespa scooter which he had bought a month before to set off for the school in Clifton. His route took him up the Whiteladies Road to a busy junction where he would turn left down Apsley Road and then left again into Pembroke Road. As he turned into Apsley Road, he was hit by a five-ton lorry which was turning right from the opposite direction. The lorry went into the right side of the scooter, crushing it and knocking Harry into the road, where he lay crouched and unmoving.

Two nurses who worked in a nearby hospital rushed to the stricken Harry's aid, as did a passing doctor. It was immediately apparent that his right leg was very badly broken. An ambulance arrived quickly to rush him to the Bristol Royal Infirmary.

As Violet's baby was due in December, the family decided to keep the news from her, but their efforts were in vain. Her nephew Paul who had heard about it on the way back from school blurted out that Uncle Harry had had an accident. However, though the news was distressing, there was consolation that it was nothing more than a broken leg, which is all that the initial reports said, although a BRI spokesman described Harry's condition as 'poor'.

Doctors at the hospital soon ascertained that Harry's injuries were considerably more serious. They told his father and brothers who had dashed to his bedside that his leg was indeed badly fractured, so much so that they considered that he would never play football again. However, Harry had failed to regain consciousness and he would have to be transferred immediately to Frenchay hospital. At midnight, surgeons there performed an emergency operation to remove a blood clot from his brain caused by a fracture to his skull. All they could do was wait to see if he would awaken from his coma. 'His physical fitness', they told reporters, 'is just about the only hope he has of pulling through.'

The hospital switchboard was jammed with anxious callers from all parts of the country desperate for news. Hospital officials issued an appeal for people not to telephone and Supporters' Club chairman Eric Godfrey allowed his home number to be printed in the paper so that he could field enquiries about Harry's condition, which he did until 11 pm. The calls began again at 8 am the following morning.

Bert Tann was not at Eastville when the news broke, but secretary John Gummow and Eric Godfrey had gone to Moor Street to lend their support to Violet and the family. Gummow told the papers that 'Mrs. Bamford had taken the news well and was bearing up'. Godfrey had made arrangements to take Violet to the hospital day or night whenever she wished and she was able to spend as much time with her husband as she could, given that she was heavily pregnant. When Tann returned to Bristol the next day he went to see Harry and told the press: 'He is desperately ill and football doesn't matter now. All we want is to see him fit and well again, looking forward to the future with the zest he always had.' The surgeons hadn't yet given up hope that he might recover and performed a minor operation on his leg to check on the setting of the broken bones.

However, as his brothers watched over him, Harry died from laceration of the brain at 2.45 pm on 31 October 1958 without ever regaining consciousness, in the very same ward in which he had often

Bristol Schools' Football Association
ESTABLISHED 1894

Hon. Treas.
D. MAHONY,
19, PERRY ROAD,
BRISTOL, 1.

Hon. Sec.
A. H. ANDREWS,
94, WEST BROADWAY,
WESTBURY-ON-TRYM,
BRISTOL,
TELEPHONE : BRISTOL 628130 (HOME)
57875 (SCHOOL)

November 3rd 1958.

J. Gummow, Esq.,
Secretary,
Bristol Rovers' F.C.,
Eastville Stadium,
Bristol, 5.

Dear Mr. Gummow,

I write to express to the officials, players and Bristol Rovers F.C. in general the sincerest sympathy of the Bristol Schools' F.A. with the club at the loss of that gentleman of sport, Harry Bamford.

We in the Schools' Association have always admired Harry and feel that he was the personification of all that we try to instil into the lads who come under our influence. His passing will leave a gap in the ranks of sportsmen and of your club in particular which it will take a long time to fill and we all of the schoolboy Soccer world in Bristol would like to associate ourselves with our friends at Eastville at this tragic time.

May the spirit of Harry Bamford continue to inspire his friends at Eastville and all parts of the country although he has hung up his boots for the last time.

Yours very sincerely,

Hon. Secretary, Bristol Schools' F.A.

Association of Football League Referees and Linesmen.
(Association Motto : "JUSTUM ET TENACEM.")

President 1958-59:
G. E. SMITH,
66, Oliphant Circle,
Halpas, Newport,
Mon.

Hon. Treasurer:
GEORGE DUTTON,
144, Emscote Road, Warwick.
Tel.: Warwick 631.

Hon. Sec.
J. S. McLOUGHLIN,
33, Knox Avenue,
Altrincham, Middlesex
Manchester.
Tel.: Middleton 4627

7, Manor Road,
Weston-s-Mare,
November 2nd. 1958.

J. Gummow, Esq.,
Bristol Rovers F.C.Ltd.,
Eastville Stadium,
Bristol.

Dear Mr Gummow,

May I, on behalf of the members of the above Association, extend to the Bristol Rovers Football Club and to Mrs Bamford our deepest sympathy in the great loss which you have both suffered by the death of that great player and sportsman Harry Bamford.

Harry by his conduct on and off the field was truly a great example to all players and will be greatly missed.

Yours sincerely,

Norman Lye.

Hon. Sec.
West of England & South Wales Section.

Two of the many letters of condolence received by Rovers

196

entertained patients with displays of head tennis and other football skills. The local papers, which had kept the public closely informed, printed tributes to 'one of the finest gentlemen of the football field'. The letters of condolence which poured into John Gummow's office at Eastville – he acknowledged every one personally – were kept by Violet. They pay testament to the regard in which Harry was held, both within the football and sporting professions and among many ordinary people. One supporter commented: 'Over the years Harry's play had endeared him to us, he stood for everything good in the game'. Another letter came from someone who had served alongside him with the Glosters in India, where he used to watch him playing for the Battalion. The Association of Football Referees praised his sportsmanship in an official letter, but one referee, Norman Taylor, wrote his own heartfelt tribute: 'I have had the privilege in refereeing many of your games since 1947… and I am sure I speak for all referees, he was always a gentleman on the field of play, indeed the game could do with many more like him'.

While there were suggestions that the new stand should be named after him, or that memorial gates should be erected at Eastville stadium, only a day after Harry's death it was announced that a 'well-known Bristol sportsman has presented a valuable trophy as a memorial to Harry Bamford. The intention is that it shall be called the Harry Bamford Memorial Trophy and that is shall be awarded annually to the Bristol footballer – amateur or professional – who, in the opinion of a panel representative of the various Association football organisations in Bristol, is the outstanding player of the year from the point of view of good sportsmanship and gentlemanly conduct both on and off the field'. The donor did not reveal their identity.

Bert Tann was personally devastated by the sudden death of the player he had come to rely on and the man he had learned to admire, his daughter Barbara later saying that it 'shook him rigid'. He was seen walking round Eastville sad-eyed and subdued. Harry's long-time manager wrote a personal tribute in the *Post* where he was not afraid to express the depths of his grief openly: 'That he will never again don the blue and white of the Rovers through such tragic circumstances is unbearable… I cannot find words to express the tribute due to Harry Bamford. It is true to say that my personal debt to him is immeasurable. He was part of all that was best in Bristol Rovers and the club grew in stature with him. A part of Bristol Rovers died with him.'

There was, however, a football match on Saturday to prepare for. It was fitting that the game at Eastville was the first Bristol derby of the season, so that supporters from both sides of the city could join together to mourn Harry and to pay their respects. Herbert Hampden Alpass, Rovers' Chairman, said that he and his fellow directors had discussed postponement, but decided that it would have been Harry's wish that the match be played. Five minutes before the start, the two teams, led out by the referee Mervyn Griffiths and the linesmen, followed by the Lord Mayor, Alderman F. G. W. Chamberlain, Mr. Vic Newman, chairman of the Gloucestershire Football Association who was in charge of the Bristol Boys team of which Harry had been a member before the war and directors and officials of both Bristol clubs, walked slowly on to the pitch. They formed two lines, while they listened solemnly to a tribute composed by John Gummow which was read out by Rovers' director John Hare:

'A great Bristolian has passed from our midst. He graced this pitch with such rare distinction and it is here, where he so loved to play his game, that all of us now assembled pay tribute in a simple, but nonetheless affectionate manner to him.

We now join together in a few moments of silence, remembering Harry Bamford for the steadfast example he always was, and for the inspiration his memory will for ever be.'

32,104 fans stood bare-headed for a minute in absolute silence, many in tears, before the players, wearing black armbands, kicked off. Spectators at Twerton Park where Bath were playing Trowbridge in the FA Cup did the same. The match itself was not dampened by Harry's death, although the crowd was noticeably more quiet than usual, Rovers pressing for an equaliser at the end but losing 2-1 because of two defensive errors.

The funeral was held at St. Mary Redcliffe, the same beautiful parish

Players and officials of Rovers and City form two lines on the pitch at Eastville to pay their respects before the Bristol derby shortly after Harry's death

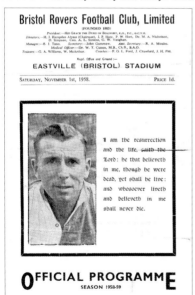

Bristol Rovers Football Club, Limited
(FOUNDED 1883)

President:—HIS GRACE THE DUKE OF BEAUFORT, K.G., P.C., G.C.V.O.
Directors:—H. J. Hampden Alpass (Chairman), J. P. Hare, P. W. Hort, Dr. M. A. Nicholson, D. Simpson, Coo. A. L. Stevens, G. W. Vaughan.
Manager:—B. J. Tann.   Secretary:—John Gummow.   Asst. Secretary:—R. A. Moules.
Medical Officer:—Dr. W. T. Cusses, M.B., Ch.B., B.A.O.
Trainers:—G. A. Williams, W. McArthur.   Coaches:—F. G. L. Ford, J. Crawford, J. H. Pitt.

Regd. Office and Ground :—

EASTVILLE (BRISTOL) STADIUM

SATURDAY, NOVEMBER 1st, 1958.   PRICE 1d.

I am the resurrection and the life, saith the Lord: he that believeth in me, though he were dead, yet shall he live: and whosoever liveth and believeth in me shall never die.

OFFICIAL PROGRAMM**E**
SEASON 1958-59

FOOTBALL LEAGUE DIVISION II.   KICK-OFF 2.45 p.m.

BRISTOL ROVERS v. BRISTOL CITY

R.   **BRISTOL ROVERS**   L.
Colours—Blue and White Quarters, White Shorts
RADFORD

DOYLE (2)   WATLING (3)

SYKES (4)   PYLE (5)   SAMPSON (6)

McILVENNY (7)   BIGGS (8)   BRADFORD (Capt.) (9)   WARD (10)   HOOPER (11)

Referee :   *Linesmen :*
Mr. B. M. GRIFFITHS (Newport)   O   Mr. F. C. CASE (Red Flag)
Mr. J. G. D. LEWIS (Yellow Flag)

WATKINS (11)   ETHERIDGE (10)   ATYEO (9)   TINDILL (8)   VIRGIN (7)

BURDEN (Capt.) (6)   WILLIAMS (5)   McCALL (4)

THRESHER (3)   HOPKINSON (2)

COOK

L.   **BRISTOL CITY**   R.
Colours—Red Shirts, White Collars, White Shorts.

Code for Half-Time Scores

Letters on Board	TEAMS	SCORES	Letters on Board	TEAMS	SCORES
A	Arsenal		K	Leyton Orient	
	Newcastle United			Huddersfield Town	
B	Birmingham City		L	Lincoln City	
	Portsmouth			Brighton	
C	Everton		M	Scunthorpe	
	Blackburn Rovers			Barnsley	
D	Leeds United		N	Sheffield Wednesday	
	Manchester United			Rotherham United	
E	Luton Town		O	Stoke City	
	Aston Villa			Liverpool	
F	Manchester City		P	Sunderland	
	Tottenham Hotspur			Grimsby Town	
G	West Bromwich Albion		R	Swansea Town	
	Wolverhampton W.			Middlesbrough	
H	Derby County		S	Chesterfield	
	Cardiff City			Plymouth Argyle	
I	Fulham		T	Swindon Town	
	Sheffield United			Reading	
J	Ipswich Town		V	Brighton & Hove Res.	
	Charlton Athletic			Bristol Rovers Res.	

The simple programme issued for that game

church on whose steps he and Violet had stood sharing their happiness with family and friends after their wedding only four years previously. On Thursday 6 November, over a thousand men and women packed the church for the ceremony, while many more stood in the churchyard and in the streets outside. Extra police had to be drafted in to control the traffic. There is a list of 150 floral tributes in the family papers which were sent to Eastville from all parts of Britain. These were laid in a corner of the north enclosure and the players and staff walked along them reading the messages, Alfie Biggs in particular visibly moved. The most impressive wreath was one in the shape of a football from Captain Arthur Prince Cox, a former manager of the club, referee and boxing promoter. The Burma Star Association sent one in the shape of a star in yellow flowers. More touching, perhaps, were the smaller, more personal remembrances; a bunch of chrysanthemums tied with a ribbon came from the boys in Lower IVB, Clark's Grammar School. Their Headmaster, Mr. Dupe, would later begin their annual prize-giving ceremony with thanks to Harry for his great help in building up the school's football teams, saying that Harry was 'admired as a footballer and a gentleman by all boys at the school'. Five cars carried the flowers and wreaths to the church. A separate list records the 56 floral tributes sent by Harry's family, friends and former team mates from the Marsh, as well as others whose lives had been touched in other ways by Harry, such as Maureen Cooper whom he once crowned Lynwell Carnival Queen. Many more brought flowers on the day.

Groups of women with babies, workmen in their overalls and others waited by the roadside to watch the cortege as it slowly wound its way to Arnos Vale Cemetery. Hilary's Uncle Tony told her later that he thought the rows of people standing on the banks beside the road resembled the terraces of Eastville. Harry was laid to rest in the family plot, alongside his old friend, Violet's first husband Harry Boon.

It is impossible to imagine what Violet was going through. But she had her unborn child to think of as well as Hilary. She had the support of the family to call on; later Harry's younger brother Alan and his wife Mavis would move into the house next door to the one that Harry had bought in Brislington. Violet donated the collection made by neighbours in St. Philip's Marsh to Frenchay Hospital as 'a token of appreciation for the great skill, care and devotion shown in the fight to save her husband's life'.

However, as Harry's death was as a result of a road accident outside of football, he did not qualify for a benefit from the Football League. As he had also spent his savings on a house, the decision was taken to launch a fund-raising appeal on behalf of Violet and her soon-to-be two daughters. 'The Harry Bamford Fund' was set up at a meeting at Eastville attended by the Rovers' Chairman and Directors, Bert Tann,

BRISTOL ROVERS' SUPPORTERS' CLUB
HARRY BAMFORD FUND

As a mark of gratitude we have much pleasure in publishing a full list of subscriptions to the above Fund.

E. W. H. GODFREY,
Chairman and Hon. Secretary.

The Harry Bamford Fund raised over £6,000.

John Gummow, who was appointed its secretary, Eric Godfrey of the Supporters Club, the sports editors of the three local papers and Mr. Goodright of the Westminster Bank to whose branches subscriptions were to be sent. Bristol Rovers opened it with a donation of £1,000, followed by £100 from the Supporters Club. Donations came from all over: Harry's team mates, professional and amateur football clubs, two schools, individual Supporters Club branches, referees' associations, the *Evening Post*, firms, sports, social and youth clubs, collections in pubs and factories, as well as many private individuals. The main fund-raising event was to be a memorial benefit game planned for the end of the season, where the Harry Bamford Memorial Trophy would be awarded for the first time.

In the meantime, the inquest into the crash which caused Harry's death returned a verdict of accidental death. The lorry driver admitted he had cut the corner turning into Apsley Road and had not seen the scooter. Another lorry waiting to turn right into Burlington Road had complicated matters and the dazzling sunlight which funnelled down Apsley Road and still today makes driving along it difficult, all contributed to what happened. Eyewitnesses stated that, in their opinion, the collision could not have been avoided.

THE HARRY BAMFORD MEMORIAL MATCH

COMBINED BRISTOL XI
v.
ARSENAL

FRIDAY, 8th MAY, 1959
Kick-off 6.45 p.m.

SOUTH STAND 5/-
"B" Block
Row **K**   Seat No. 54
THIS PORTION TO BE RETAINED.

IN THE EVENT OF POSTPONEMENT, TICKETS AVAILABLE ON RE-ARRANGED DATE; NO MONEY REFUNDED.

Ticket for the Memorial match between a Bristol XI of Rovers and City players and Arsenal which swelled the Fund considerably

Perfect weather greeted the Memorial match on Friday, 8 May 1959, when a team composed of players from both Rovers and City took on Arsenal. The 28,347 gate was a record for a friendly game at Eastville and admission and car parking fees and sales of programmes for 3d apiece (as well as Arsenal waiving their expenses) meant that £3,709 6s and 6d was added to The Harry Bamford Fund, swelling it to over £6,000 – more than £1,000 above the original target. The match itself was 'a magnificent exhibition of football', which Arsenal initially seemed to be taking a little too easily, Geoff Bradford opening the scoring on eight minutes, before Atyeo claimed the second and Bradford added another. This woke Arsenal up and the half ended 3-2 to Bristol. More goals followed after the break, the Bristol XI finally triumphing 5-4, both teams warmly applauded off at the end.

Immediately after the final whistle, John Gummow asked for silence over the public address system and thanked Bristol and the West Country for the magnificent turn-out. He went on: 'Mrs. Bamford has particularly requested me to convey to you her sincere gratitude…'

He then revealed the identity of the winner of The Harry Bamford Trophy – a surprised and delighted Geoff Bradford – to loud applause.

'Geoff,' he continued, 'has graced the game here in Bristol with great distinction… twice his courage has triumphed over the adversity of the severest of injuries. Not once in the 357 games in which he has played in the colours of Bristol Rovers has a referee ever had the occasion to question his conduct.

'Off the field of play it would be difficult indeed to imagine anyone so unassuming and so modest of his own achievements. Like his great friend Harry Bamford there is nothing unkind in his personality and, like Harry Bamford too he will be remembered with affection by generations of Bristolians.' Later Violet presented Geoff with the trophy and a certificate and attended the dinner organised by the Duke of Beaufort at which the players were presented with a gold propelling pencil by the Duke.

Violet kept the letter which John Gummow sent to her after the game in which he professed himself 'thrilled' and admitted he found it an 'emotional experience'. On 20 December 1960, Gummow unexpectedly resigned as Rovers' secretary, the post which he had filled for so long and with such dedication, citing the stress of the job as the reason. Three years later, the *Evening Post* revealed that Gummow, who was working in London for Harvey and Sons, had written to the Harry Bamford Memorial Trophy selection committee to reveal that he was the anonymous donor. What prompted him to do this is not clear. What is certain, however, is that John Gummow had a deep and abiding admiration for Harry Bamford which pre-dated his time at Bristol Rovers. The opening chapter of this book quoted passages of a letter to George Baker of the *Evening World* from an anonymous admirer who had followed Harry since his schoolboy days, detailing his sporting achievements in India. At the age of 17, Gummow had become secretary of Kingswood AFC, his local District League soccer team, before spending seven years in the British Army in Egypt and the Indian Army in Burma, where he had been the Regimental Sergeant

Harry's death touched many outside Bristol

Major appointed to accompany Tommy Walker's touring International Football XI. It seems highly likely that keen statistician John Gummow was the person who had written to the paper to sing Harry's praises at the start of his career and was now seeking to preserve Harry's memory and ensure that his conduct and achievements would inspire future generations.

CHAPTER 14

The End of a Golden Age

Violet's and Harry's second daughter, Julie, was born on 7 December 1958. Life for Violet after Harry's death was far from easy. The Harry Bamford Fund of over £6,000 was not handed over to her, but administered as a trust by Rovers' Chairman Herbert Hampden Alpass who was also a solicitor and another Rovers' director. Violet received a small monthly sum from the fund, but had to go out to work full time to support her family. Her eldest daughter Hilary remembers her Mum worrying about telephoning the rather stern Rovers' chairman to ask for an extra payment to replace their broken washing machine. The remaining money in the fund was eventually turned over to the family after Hampden Alpass's death in 1999. Violet never remarried and passed away in 2006. As her eldest daughter Hilary revealed in her Foreword to this book, the family had to cope with yet another crushing tragedy when Julie was killed aged 16 in a road accident in Wales.

Bert Tann and John Gummow became the first Chairman and Honourable Secretary respectively of the Friends of Frenchay Hospital, where the surgeons and nurses had fought to save Harry's life. Gummow, as we have seen, suddenly left his job at Rovers in 1960, because, he said, he was unable to cope with the stress any longer, and went to work in London, to be replaced as Rovers' secretary by his assistant Ron Moules. When Ron Moules died suddenly in 1968, Bert Tann who had been replaced as Rovers' manager by his one-time assistant Fred Ford, became Rovers' General Manager and Club Secretary. Tann died of a heart attack in 1972 aged 58, having worked tirelessly for Rovers and many charities in his adopted city.

After Harry's death, Bristol Rovers initially continued to finish in the top half of the Second Division, sixth in 1959 and ninth in 1960.

The family outside the house in Broomhill which Harry bought shortly before his death. At the front from the left are Julie and Hilary (who remembers that her dress was bright pink crimplene and she hated it). Grandmothers Daisy Bamford and Violet Holvey are at the back, along with a family friend

However, Bert Tann's new team of young local talent was relegated to the Third Division in 1962 after nine seasons in the Second Division, bringing to an end what is generally accepted as a – if not the – golden age of Rovers' history. The following season, Rovers narrowly escaped a consecutive relegation to the Fourth Division. Josser Watling played left-back for Bristol Rovers until he retired in 1963, having made 323 League appearances since joining Rovers in 1945, the same year as Harry.

After playing what was his final match for Rovers, his 486th Football League appearance at Derby County on 3 September 1958, Harry was Rovers' all-time record appearance holder. At the time, aged 38 years 209 days, he was the third oldest to have played for the club. Harry's remarkable record remained until Stuart Taylor, who in March 1980 ended his career with 546 appearances, surpassed it

If he had not been involved in that terrible accident, would Harry Bamford have played on for another two seasons as he hoped? Very possibly, and he may also have made a few more appearances in the first team when needed. He would, without doubt, have continued to do his bit in the Reserves to bring on young players. Violet told Hilary later that Harry had been offered a job coaching football in Australia and was keen to start a new life in the country he had admired so much when he toured there in 1951. Violet was not so sure; she didn't want to leave Bristol and family when she had a small child and Harry understood her reasons. So it is likely that Harry's future would have involved coaching young footballers in local schools and on courses for the Somerset and Gloucestershire FA and perhaps even working as a coach at Eastville. Instead, he has passed into Rovers' folklore, fondly remembered by team mates and fans alike as a wonderful player, a one club man and, as one of his obituaries so aptly put it, one of the pre-eminent exponents of his day of the sportsmanship to which everyone should aspire, Bristol soccer's 'First Gentleman of Football'.

Harry proudly displays his caps and medals

Harry Bamford
Playing Career and Honours

Schoolboy Football Honours

- Woodcock Shield Winner's medals with St. Silas School 1932, 1933 & 1934
- Bristol and South Gloucestershire Schools League Shield Winner's medal 1933
- Bristol Boys' Caps 1931-32, 1932-33, 1933-34

Bristol Rovers

1945-46

Appearances (all competitions): 19	Goals: 4

1946-59

Appearances		Goals
League:	486	5
FA Cup	38	0
Gloucestershire Cup	9	0
Total:	533	5

Rovers' statistics taken from Mike Jay, *Bristol Rovers F.C.: A Complete Record 1883-1987* (Breedon, 1987)

Honours

- England 'B' Cap, Tour of Australia 1951
- Four Gloucestershire Senior Cup Winner's Medals, 1948, 1949, 1955, 1956
- Division III South Championship Winner's Medal 1953

THE HARRY BAMFORD MEMORIAL TROPHY

Introduction by Steve Sutor

The Box in the Rovers' Storeroom: The Rediscovery of the Harry Bamford Memorial Trophy

Throughout the 1960s, the Harry Bamford Memorial Trophy was perhaps the premier award for footballers in Bristol. Every year, a panel selected the winner from a list of nominations drawn from the professional and amateur ranks, 'the outstanding player of the year from the point of view of good sportsmanship and gentlemanly conduct both on and off the field'. Then, in 1974, the presentations stopped. While researching my previous book, *Every Schoolboy's Dream: The History of the Woodcock Shield*, I had the privilege of meeting up with Harry Bamford's daughter Hilary Lewis and her husband Geoff at their home, where they kindly supplied me with photographs and clippings for the book about Hilary's dad, who had won the Shield twice in the early 1930s as part of the St Silas school team. There were many clippings about the Memorial Trophy, but Hilary had not been able to find out why it stopped being awarded and had been told that it had been destroyed in the Eastville Stand fire in 1980.

Hilary and I discussed reviving the Trophy in honour of her dad's memory and I decided to make a replica. I carved one from oak and Gary Hillard, the son of Doug Hillard who was one of Harry Bamford's understudies at Rovers and sometimes roomed with him for away matches, engraved the names of the winners from 1958-1973 on it. Then I received a call from Rod Wesson, Bristol Rovers' Secretary, with whom I had been in regular contact about reviving the award. He could hardly contain his excitement. 'Harold [Jarman] has found a box of trophies in the Bristol Rovers' storeroom - and the original Bamford

Hilary with Rovers' legend Harold Jarman, who found the cardboard box of trophies lost for 40 years

Trophy is one of them!' I rushed to the Mem. There was the Trophy, heavily tarnished as it hadn't seen the light of day for forty years, but unmistakeable. Rod allowed me to take it home and clean it.

Since the polish revealed the name of the first holder, Geoff Bradford, to this day the only Rovers man to have played for England while at the club, I have been tracking down the past winners and inviting nominations from the public on social media for those years in which the Trophy had lain unseen in its box. In the interests of fairness, it was decided that there should be an equal number of Bristol Rovers and City players, 13, and 14 local clubmen, in the spirit of the original intentions of its donor. The Mem and Ashton Gate have hosted the presentations which have received a warm reception from fans and the wider Bristol public.

Acknowledgments

First and foremost, I would like to thank Joyce Woolridge for all the time and effort she has spent putting this wonderful story together. This book would not have been written without her. It has also been an honour and a privilege working with Harry's daughter Hilary and her husband Geoff Lewis on all the 40 presentations of the Harry Bamford Trophy.

Bristol Rovers and Bristol City have been very accommodating and kind at all the awards with Nick Day and David Lloyd doing a marvellous job announcing on the pitch. Also, thanks to Marina Dolman Bristol City's President and Nick Higgs, former Bristol Rovers' Chairman, who gave their time with the presentations. The hospitality shown to us by the staff at both clubs was second to none, especially Ron Cocks and Mike Locke at Rovers, as was chatting with Josser Watling and Harold Jarman about Harry and their memories before the game!

Thanks also for all the help from Rovers historians Mike Jay and Keith Brookman, and for the media coverage from Don Veale at the *Sunday Independent* and Dan Newman at the *Bristol Post*. I am indebted to former Rovers' Secretary Rod Wesson for his help finding the Trophy and his successor Dave Sams.   ***Steve Sutor***

Trophy's back after 40-year gap, and will honour 40 football heroes

Steve Sutor, with a replica Harry Bamford Memorial Trophy which will be presented to Harry Bamford's daughter who was threee when he died, John Honeyfield, who won the trophy in 1971 playing St Aldhelm's, and Rod Wessson, secretary of Rovers FC wuth the Junior Trophy. (Picture: John Kent). Bristol Post, 9 -11 May 2014

The Harry Bamford
Memorial Trophy

The previous chapter explained how John Gummow, Secretary of Bristol Rovers, anonymously donated the Harry Bamford Memorial Trophy in November 1958 and then revealed his identity in a letter to the selection committee in 1963, reminding them of the criteria for awarding it, to 'perpetuate his name and the ideals he championed' but also to inspire all those who played football in Bristol, amateur and professional, to emulate Harry's sportsmanship and dedication. Gummow went on: 'The example he set is very clear, yet not easy to attain: wholehearted dedication to the game, high standards of perfection through constant practice; ensuring that physical fitness was not marred by tempting diversions; above all, never stooping to untoward conduct. Difficult targets? Indeed they are, but not quite impossible, for one player managed all these attainments.'

Geoff Bradford, goalscorer supreme and a one-club man who turned down a move to Liverpool, was the natural, but surprised first recipient. As John Gummow announced to the crowd at the Memorial match between a Combined Bristol XI and Arsenal on 9 May 1959, 'Not once in the 357 games he has played in the colours of Bristol Rovers' has a referee ever had occasion to question his conduct'. Violet Bamford presented him with the trophy and a framed certificate afterwards.

In subsequent years, nominations from the public were invited, to be sent to the *Evening Post* Sports' Editor who was part of the selection committee, which initially also included Bert Tann, the Chairmen of both professional Bristol clubs, City's Harry Dolman and Rovers'

Violet Bamford presents the Trophy for the first time to Harry's close friend and team mate Geoff Bradford in 1959

Hampden Alpass, A.V. Newman, the Chair of the Gloucestershire Football Association and Bill Pinnell, the retired *Evening Post* football writer 'The Traveller'. The presentations usually took place at the annual Gloucestershire Senior Professional Cup match contested by Rovers and City, when the previous holder would pass the Trophy on to his successor.

The first amateur to receive the Trophy, from Geoff Bradford after a friendly match against Swedish club Djurgarden in March 1960, was talented all-rounder Colin Mitchell, whose prowess at both football (as captain of Clifton St. Vincent's) and cricket received regular coverage in the local papers. A modest, unassuming gentleman, Colin became a popular teacher at Brislington School, which both Harry Bamford's daughters, Hilary and Julie attended.

Bob Anderson, the Bristol City goalkeeper who once played for Rovers, was the next name to be engraved on the trophy, but as he was in hospital having surgery for a spinal injury, his wife had to stand in for him when it was handed over in 1961 to Bert Britton, secretary of Avonmouth FC who had been playing for the club for 31 years since he was 15 and still managed the occasional game at the age of 46. Albert Allen, player and chairman of Parson Street Old Boys AFC (1963) presented the Trophy to one of Bristol City's greatest ever players, John Atyeo in 1964.

The certificate which accompanied the Trophy was proudly displayed in Bristol Rovers' long-serving wing-half Ray Mabbutt's home until his death in 2016, demonstrating what an honour professionals and amateurs alike considered being awarded the Trophy to be. Amateur Jack King (1966), who played for and skippered Hanham Athletic for 13 years, Jack Connor (1967), Bristol City centre-half and defensive anchor throughout the 1960s, Burt Biggs of St. Philip's Marsh Adult School (1968) brother of Rovers' star Alfie and Harold Jarman (1969), Rovers' wonder winger and Gloucestershire cricketer, completed the roll of honour in the 1960s.

Presentations to Terry Bush, one-club forward for Bristol City (1970), amateur John Honeyfield of St Aldhelms FC (1971), long-serving Rovers' forward and another team mate of Harry Bamford, Bobby Jones (1972) and Soundwell FC's full-back Ray Bean (1973), who, as we have seen, had fond memories of Harry's kindness to a nervous young player, and made over 500 appearances for the amateur club, ushered in the new decade.

Ray Bean was to be the final recipient of the Trophy until its revival in 2013. In 1972, Bert Tann, then Rovers' general manager and secretary, who still chaired the selection committee, told the *Evening Post* that he felt that the Trophy 'could now be best used as the championship prize for a Bristol area junior league'. Nothing, he stressed, would be done without the approval of Harry's widow, Violet, and the award 'has been richly prized by the people who have won it'. But, Tann, argued, the Trophy no longer had the same significance with the younger generation as a decade ago. Bert Tann died suddenly in 1972, which probably explains why these plans were not followed through. Ray Bean was left holding the Trophy for fifteen months, before Rovers asked him to return it.

The modern presentation certificate

Geoff Bradford passes the Trophy on to local amateur club Clifton St. Vincent's captain Colin Mitchell in March 1960 after a friendly game between Rovers and Swedish club Djurgarden

Bob Anderson, goalkeeper for both Rovers and City (1954-1959) was awarded the Trophy in 1961

Bert Britton, secretary of Avonmouth FC, smiles as Mrs Bob Anderson hands him the Trophy on behalf of her husband in 1962 while Ron Moules, Rovers' secretary, looks on

Albert Allen, former player and chairman of Parson Street Old Boys AFC in Bedminster (1963), shown here handing over the Trophy to Bristol City's John Atyeo

John Atyeo (1964), whose 645 appearances (1951-1966) and record 351 goals, as well as six England caps, made him a Bristol City legend. Harry, along with the rest of the Rovers' defence, had many a tussle with 'Big John'

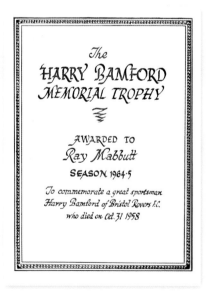

The
HARRY BAMFORD
MEMORIAL TROPHY

AWARDED TO
Ray Mabbutt

SEASON 1964-5

To commemorate a great sportsman
Harry Bamford of Bristol Rovers F.C.
who died on Oct. 31 1958

Ray Mabbutt's original certificate, designed and made by the Evening Post's Art Editor, which Ray kept on display in his home for more than 50 years

Ray Mabbutt, wing-half for Rovers from 1957-1969, another team mate of Harry and father of future Rovers' and Spurs' star Gary, holder of the Trophy for 1965, presents it in 1966 to Hanham Athletic's Jack King 'a fine example of an amateur footballer who has never been disciplined on the field'

Jack Connor (left), centre-half and defensive mainstay for Bristol City (1960-1971), is delighted to receive the award from Jack King in 1967. Connor's cheerful manner and wholehearted approach endeared him to City fans

A dapper Burt Biggs, who played for amateur club St. Philip's Marsh Adult School, first formed in 1919, poses with the Trophy in 1968 in the garden of the house where he still lives

Bristol-born Harold Jarman, who delighted Rovers' fans for fourteen years (1959-1973) with his tricky wing play and is the club's third highest scorer as well as playing cricket for Gloucestershire, holding the trophy in 1969 alongside Burt Biggs and Rovers' director Gordon Milne. Harold went on to manage Rovers from 1979-80

Forward Terry Bush, a one club man for Bristol City from 1960 onwards, was awarded the Trophy in 1970, the year he was forced to retire through injury

John Honeyfield of amateur club St. Aldhelm's FC from Bedminster is presented with the Trophy in 1971 by the previous year's winner Terry Bush at Eastville. Bert Tann, chair of the selection committee, seems to be enjoying the occasion. John is now President of Headley Park FC

Long-serving, speedy forward Bristolian Bobby Jones, a team mate of Harry's, who played for Rovers in two spells from 1957-67 and 1968-73, beams as he displays the Trophy in 1972

The final original Trophy holder, Ray Bean, whose 500 appearances for amateur club Soundwell made him a deserving recipient in 1973. Ray was on Rovers' books for five years as an amateur and has never forgotten Harry's kindness to him

The Junior Harry Bamford Memorial Trophy

On the morning 31 October 1968, the ten year anniversary of Harry Bamford's death, a parcel, marked 'Handle With Care' awaited the staff who arrived for work at the Eastville offices. Mrs. Marjorie Hall, Bert Tann's secretary, opened it to find an impressive trophy inscribed, 'The Junior Harry Bamford Trophy'. An unsigned letter inside the box explained that the trophy was intended to be presented annually at the same time as the senior award to the local professional or amateur footballer under 21 'who most nearly approaches the example set by Harry Bamford as decided by an appropriate selection committee'.

The anonymous donor (who was not John Gummow) had, the letter said, obtained Violet Bamford's permission to use Harry's name and paid this tribute to Harry:

'He was a professional footballer in the truest sense of the word. Dedicated and sincere, his qualities invariably shone through to make him a fine example. He was like a piece of pure gold, a footballer so proud of his craft that he would never do anything that might tarnish it'.

The Junior Trophy was only presented three times: to John Tanner in 1969, Keith Milsom of Sneyd Park FC in 1970, and Dave Hall in 1971. It seems there might have been a problem in securing nominations from local clubs. Despite an attempt by the donor to widen the scope of the award by suggesting in a letter to Chris Wilcox of the Bristol Federation of Boys' Clubs in February 1970 that a representative of the Bristol Schools' Football Association might be included on the panel of judges and nominations invited from schools, Dave Hall was left literally holding the trophy – for 42 years.

John Tanner of Bedminster Down Boys' Club, the first recipient of the new Junior Trophy, poses alongside Harold Jarman, who received the Senior Trophy, on the pitch at Eastville

John Tanner passes the Junior Trophy on to Keith Milsom of Sneyd Park FC in 1970. Also in the photo is Brian Stone of Sneyd Park, who nominated Keith for the award

Dave Hall, little realising that he would be in possession of the Junior Trophy for the next 42 years, takes his award from Keith Milsom at Eastville in 1971

Dave Hall presents the Junior Trophy to Brad Hardidge in 2015, flanked by the then Rovers' Chairman Nick Higgs and the other previous holders John Tanner and Keith Milsom at the Memorial Stadium

The 'Fabulous Forty'
The Senior Trophy is Revived

For the next seven years, the senior Harry Bamford Trophy stood disregarded in the trophy room at Eastville, until the catastrophic events of 1980. A '£1 million blaze' left Bristol Rovers' South stand in ruins. Rovers' apprentices including Ian Holloway and Keith Curle as well as manager Terry Cooper took part in the salvage operation, packing some valuables into a cardboard box. The heat of the fire was so intense that the golden boot trophy awarded to the club's youth team in Holland during that summer's tour melted and it was believed that the Harry Bamford Trophy had suffered the same fate.

My introduction tells the story of how Harry's daughter Hilary made inquiries about the trophy in 2008 and was told that it could not be found and had probably been destroyed in the fire. Both Hilary and I continued the search, until I received the phone call telling me that Harold Jarman had found a battered cardboard box of dusty trophies in a storeroom at the Memorial Ground with the Harry Bamford Trophy among them.

I wanted to revive the award and it was decided to invite nominations on social media for 40 Bristol sportsmen, 13 Rovers' professionals, 13 City professionals and 14 local club players to fill the gaps left since 1973. The presentations at both the Memorial Stadium and Ashton Gate have been given a warm response by officials and fans of both clubs, who have been able to celebrate the achievements of past professional heroes and those amateurs who have given their time to the grassroots of the game. For those awarded the Trophy who, sadly, are no longer with us, there has been the opportunity for their proud families to commemorate them.

The former Bristol City players honoured are: Louis Carey, Jantzen

Derrick, Brian Drysdale, Chris Garland, Mike Gibson, Jimmy Mann, Julian Marshall, Geoff Merrick, Scott Murray, Dave Rodgers, Gerry Sweeney, Trevor Tainton, Brian Tinnion and Alan Walsh.

The Bristol Rovers players are: Mickey Barrett, Bruce Bannister, Alfie Biggs, Doug Hillard, Ian Holloway, Phil Kite, Gary Mabbutt, Frankie Prince, Paul Randall, Dick Sheppard, Stuart Taylor, Geoff Twentyman and Steve Yates.

Three recipients, Pete Aitken, Trevor Jacobs and Steve Phillips, played for both Rovers and City.

The amateur players awarded the Trophy are Phil Brake (Brislington), Mike Fox (Chipping Sodbury), Bob Fudge (Nicholas Wanderers), John Gibbs (Longwell

Doug Hillard, Bristol Rovers' right-back from 1958-68 and Harry's long-term replacement. Doug was told to sit next to Harry on Rovers' team coach to learn all he could about the art of being a full-back

Green), Terry Hardwell (Backwell United), Rusty Jacobs (Parson Street Old Boys), Roy James (Old Georgians), Tony Mattocks (Ashton United), Jeff Meacham (Brislington), Terry Mitchell (Cadbury Heath), George Philipou (Lebeq Tavern) Kenny Phillips (Dundry Athletic), Tony Ricketts (Bath City), Owen Smith (Lebeq Tavern) and Keith Swift (Highridge United).

The first presentation to a member of the 'Fabulous Forty' was to the late Doug Hilliard which was accepted on his behalf by his son Gary. This was entirely fitting as Doug became Rovers' long-term replacement for Harry Bamford at right-back.

Gary Hillard accepts the Trophy and certificate on behalf of his late father Doug from Ray Bean, the last holder in 1972. Next to Ray is Harry's daughter, Hilary Lewis

Trevor Jacobs' grandson Marcus proudly holds high a photograph of the late tough-tackling right back who played for Bristol City from 1965-72 and then helped Rovers win promotion to the Second Division in May 1973. Trevor's wife Mary, having received the Trophy from Bristol City's President Marina Dolman MBE, is delighted by the applause at Ashton Gate

Daughters Juliet and Melanie and grandchildren Amber, Harry, Phoebe, Alfred and Ella of Harry's late team mate Alfie Biggs receive the Trophy on his behalf. Knowle West's Alfie, with 199 goals in 473 League games between 1953 and 1969, remains Rovers' second top goal scorer of all time

Alfie Biggs, the 'Baron of Eastville'

(L – R) Keith Swift (Highridge United), Tony Mattocks (Plough & Windmill), Kenny Phillips (Dundry Athletic) & Brian Drysdale (Bristol City) enjoy their lap of honour at Ashton Gate. Aside from his long association with Dundry United, Ken Phillips assisted City's schoolboy and youth set up for 16 years.

Jantzen Derrick, Bristol City winger (1959-71) who also played for Paris St-Germain, accepts the Trophy from Rusty Jacobs (Parson Street Old Boys). Also honoured was Keith Swift (far left), coach and secretary for Highridge United for more than 25 years

Bristol-born winger Mickey Barrett played 129 games for Rovers before his life was tragically cut short by cancer aged just 24 in 1984.

Mickey Barrett's son, Liam, born six weeks after his father's death, wife Louise and grandson Charlie accept the Trophy on his behalf at the Mem, alongside Hilary Lewis and Steve Sutor

Bristol Rovers' Alan Warboys (back right) and Bruce Bannister (front right), famed for their goal-scoring exploits as the 'Smash and Grab' forward line of the 1970s, pick up their award. Celebrating with them (clockwise from front left) are John Gibbs (Longwell Green) and Peter Aitken, Alan Walsh (Bristol City) and Stuart Taylor (Bristol Rovers). Peter Aitken was a committed and uncompromising defensive midfielder with Rovers between 1972 and 1980. During a short spell at Bristol City he became one of the Ashton Gate Eight. From 2000, for 16 seasons as Community Officer he oversaw the establishment of the Bristol Rovers Community Trust.

John Gibbs has been associated with Longwell Green Sports AFC for 40 years both as a successful player and player-manager. He is now Chairman of one of the biggest amateur clubs in the South West, working tirelessly to fundraise and further establish both the adult and junior sections. John was thrilled to receive the Trophy alongside his heroes Alan Warboys and Bruce Bannister.

Former Bristol Rovers' striker (1986-88) Jeff Meacham takes time out from successfully managing Brislington FC to receive the Trophy from Hilary Lewis. After 16 years, he recently stepped down from his managerial duties, but, such is the esteem in which he is held, was persuaded to stay on as Director of Football.

After first starting playing for Brislington FC in his teens, Phil Brake has served the club in many different roles. In the 1990s, during his tenure as Vice Chairman, he championed the club's successful application for promotion to the Western League. A respected figure at the club, Phil even lends a hand behind the bar on matchdays.

Centre-half Stuart Taylor, local-born one club man (1965-1980) holds the record, 546, for the most League appearances for Bristol Rovers, breaking Harry's previous record of 486 games. Stuart, a regular at Rovers' home games, receives the Trophy from former Rovers' chairman Nick Higgs

Co-founding members of Lebeq Tavern George Philipou and Owen Smith receive their awards in recognition of their 30 year association with the successful Easton club. The Trophy rests in the safe hands of former City (1997-2006) and Rovers (2006-10) goalkeeper Steve Phillips

Wife Jill and former team mate Kelvin Grainger, holding a photograph of his clubmate, receive the Trophy on behalf of the late Roy James of Old Georgians who Kelvin tried unsuccesfully to revive when he collapsed during a game

Tony Mattocks takes a bow at Ashton Gate in recognition of his 40 plus years of service for Plough and Windmill United, now Ashton United

'Eight Men Had a Dream': four of the 'Ashton Gate Eight', forced to tear up their contracts in 1982 to ensure the continued survival of Bristol City, (L-R) Geoff Merrick, Gerry Sweeney, Julian Marshall and, on behalf of Chris Garland (1966-71), his brother Martyn line up at Ashton Gate. The other four were Pete Aitken (pictured earlier), Jimmy Mann (1974-82), Dave Rodgers and Trevor Tainton

Bristolian Geoff Merrick, inspirational Bristol City captain and central defender (1967-1982) is flanked by his twin sons Luke and Elliot

Trevor Tainton, long-serving Bristol City midfielder with 486 League appearances and a regular in City's First Division team shares a smile with Marina Dolman at his presentation

Bristol-born Dave Rodgers, central defender for Bristol City (1969-82) and one of the Ashton Gate Eight

Another of the Ashton Gate Eight, Jimmy Mann was a skilful attacking midfielder who made 231 appearances for the Robins from 1974-82

Chris Garland, forward for Bristol City in two spells between 1966 and 1971 & 1976 and 1983 making 207 League appearances and one of the Ashton Gate Eight after playing for Chelsea and Leicester. Chris is pictured here with the Woodcock Shield which he won as a schoolboy in 1962

The late Dick Sheppard's wife Chris and son Martin with Rovers' director Barry Bradshaw. Dick's grandchildren Ella and Ciaran hold a photo of the Bristol-born Rovers' goalkeeper (1969-75) toasting Rovers' success from the Watney Cup in 1972

Gerry Sweeney (centre) Bristol City midfielder, made 406 appearances from 1971-82. Tony Hardwell (right) accepted the Trophy on behalf of his late father Terry. With them is Don Veale (left) the Sunday Indy sports writer who was a good friend of Terry

The late Terry Hardwell, physio for Frome, Bath City and Backwell FC

As a winger, Scott Murray played for Bristol City between 2004 and 2009, but since then has returned to the club to serve as a youth coach and kit manager

Mike Fox, manager and sponsor of Chipping Sodbury FC, receives the Trophy in recognition of his continued support of the club

Paul Randall, Bristol Rovers' striker from 1977-78 and 1980-86 who was so popular that fans raised £55,000 to bring him back to Rovers from Stoke City

Tony Ricketts, who played 700 games at conference level and was coach and manager at Bath City, is presented with the Trophy by then Chairman of Rovers Nick Higgs. Tony also was assistant manager at Rovers and led Rovers' women's team to the League title

Former captain and defender Louis Carey, who holds the record for the highest number of League appearances, 646, for Bristol City, surpassing John Atyeo, receives the Trophy from Jantzen Derrick at the Three Lions pub in Bedminster

Bristolian Steve Yates, an integral part of Rovers' defence from 1988-1993, also served as coach and kit manager at the Mem

'Having a Gas': former Rovers' defender (1986-93) and radio broadcaster Geoff Twentyman gets a surprise live on air from Hilary and Steve

Frankie Prince, who made 362 League appearances for Rovers between 1967 and 1980 and was Community Officer for Torquay United, shakes hand with Nick Higgs at the Mem

Rusty Jacobs displays his award in recognition of his 1,342 games for Parson's Street Old Boys, the club restarted by his father after the war which Rusty has been associated with from the age of 14

Alan Walsh, striker and exponent of the 'Walshy shuffle' for Bristol City from 1984-89, makes receiving the Trophy a family occasion. Walsh coached for 11 years at City before joining Rovers as a youth coach

Hilary is joined by her daughter Jessica, Harry Bamford's granddaughter, to present the Trophy to Bob Fudge. Bob, also a recipient of an FA 50 year long service award, has served Hanham's Nicholas Wanderers as a player, reserve team manager, chairman and treasurer in his long association with the club

Boyhood Pirates' fan Phil Kite, who realised a dream when he signed as a goalkeeper for Rovers in 1980 and also served the club as goal-keeping coach and physiotherapist, receives the Trophy from Rovers' director Barry Bradshaw at his testimonial game

Iconic Bristol City midfielder Brian Tinnion, who made 458 League appearances between 1993-2005 and also managed the club, receives his award to loud cheers at Ashton Gate, where he is Director of Youth recruitment

Cadbury's Heath's President Terry Mitchell overcome with emotion as receives his award in recognition of his long association with the club. It was at Cadbury Heath's ground that Ian Holloway met his future wife, Terry's daughter Kim

Ian 'Ollie' Holloway, former Bristol Rovers' midfielder and manager, as well as managing at six other clubs, accepts the Trophy from Phil Kite

Brian 'Speedy' Drysdale who made 282 League appearances at left-back for Bristol City between 1969 and 1971, is congratulated on his award by Keith Swift

Mike Gibson, Bristol City's goalkeeper, who made 331 League appearances between 1963 and 1972, keeps Hilary and the Trophy safely in his grasp at Ashton Gate where he has also served as a goalkeeping coach for many years

Gary Mabbutt (MBE), whose late father Ray was awarded the Trophy in 1965, makes it a family double. Bristolian Gary, a Rovers, Spurs and England international defender, made 131 League appearances for Rovers between 1979-82

What better way to end than with the recipient of the Trophy in 2017, West Country Treasure John 'Josser' Watling, a Bristolian and one club man like his team mate Harry Bamford, serving Bristol Rovers for twenty years between 1945 and 1963. 93-year-old Josser still goes to every home game and has lost none of his famous sense of humour and love of a joke

Harry Bamford

October 8, 1920 - October 31, 1958

Harry goes all out to stop City's John Atyeo while Jackie Pitt looks on in the Bristol derby at Eastville on 19 January 1952 which Rovers won 2-0